Transcending Trauma

The R.E.S.T. Method for Releasing Pain, Reclaiming Perspective, and Rebuilding Meaning

by

CHRISTIAN R. BROWN

R.E.S.T. is not about doing nothing. It is about slowing trauma's urgency long enough to respond differently.

A Note Before You Begin

This book is written as an educational and reflective guide. It is not a replacement for therapy, crisis care, medical care, psychiatric care, or individualized trauma treatment. Trauma can affect the body, memory, identity, relationships, and a person's sense of safety in profound ways. Some reflections or exercises may bring up strong emotions. Move slowly. Pause when needed. Return to grounding before continuing.

If you are experiencing thoughts of self-harm, feel unsafe, are in immediate danger, or are living with ongoing abuse or coercive control, seek immediate support from emergency services, a crisis line, a trusted professional, or a safe person in your community. Healing work should never require you to face more than your body and mind can safely hold at one time.

How to move through this book safely

- Read in short sections when the material feels emotionally activating.

- Use the Release practices before attempting deeper reflection.

- Skip exercises that feel overwhelming and return to them later with support.

- Treat every reflection as an invitation, not a requirement.

- Seek professional support when trauma responses feel intense, persistent, dissociative, or unsafe.

How to Use This Book

Transcending Trauma is organized around the R.E.S.T. Method, a four-part pathway for working with the story pain leaves behind. The method begins with emotional regulation, moves into time-based perspective, helps the reader choose what deserves emotional energy, and ends with meaning reconstruction. The goal is not to erase the past. The goal is to change how the past lives inside the larger story of the self.

The R.E.S.T. Method at a Glance

- Release: Calm the emotional charge of trauma so you can respond instead of react.

- Examine Through Time: Look at pain beyond the intensity of the present moment.

- Select What Matters: Let go of what trauma taught you to carry and return your energy to what truly matters.

- Transform Meaning: Build a life story where trauma is part of what happened, not the whole of who you are.

You can read this book straight through, or you can use it as a practice guide. When a chapter feels personally relevant, slow down. Use the end-of-chapter practice pages. Write honestly, but gently. Trauma recovery does not require forcing disclosure, reliving the worst moments, or turning pain into a performance. The work here is quieter: notice what trauma taught you, test whether it is still true, and begin building a life beyond the beliefs pain left behind.

Contents

About the Author

Christian R. Brown is an author, behavioral specialist, and model developer whose work focuses on understanding the deeper stories beneath trauma, distress, and complex behavior. His writing is shaped by frontline experience with high-complexity care environments, youth and family support systems, crisis response, and the development of practical frameworks for emotional understanding and behavioral change.

Transcending Trauma reflects Christian's belief that trauma recovery requires more than revisiting what happened. It requires a way to understand how pain shaped identity, how fear reshaped perception, how emotional overload narrowed possibility, and how meaning can be rebuilt without minimizing the wound. The R.E.S.T. Method was created to give readers a clear, grounded pathway for releasing emotional intensity, reclaiming perspective, choosing what truly matters, and rebuilding a life story beyond pain.

Introduction: The Story Trauma Leaves Behind

Introduction

Trauma, in its most insidious form, is not merely an event that happens to us. It's something that we internalize, something that slowly works its way into the very core of our beliefs about ourselves and the world. It rewrites our understanding of safety, trust, and self-worth. Trauma tells us that because something terrible happened to us, we are somehow deserving of pain. It becomes a whisper in the back of our minds, a constant undercurrent of self-doubt and fear.

This internalization of trauma is what makes its impact so profound and so difficult to escape. The initial event or series of events that cause trauma may only last moments, but the effects reverberate throughout the survivor's life, often for years or even decades. Trauma becomes not just a memory of something that happened but a lens through which survivors come to view themselves and the world around them. It doesn't simply affect a person's past; it colors their present and darkens their vision for the future.

The narratives that trauma creates are often subtle at first. They might begin as fleeting thoughts - "Maybe I wasn't strong enough," or "Perhaps I deserved what happened to me." Over time, these thoughts grow roots, embedding themselves deep in the survivor's psyche until they shape their perception of reality. The pain and confusion of the traumatic event slowly morph into a distorted belief system. What was once an external circumstance becomes internalized self-blame, shame, and a fractured sense of self.

This process of internalization is particularly damaging because it goes largely unnoticed, especially in the early stages. What starts as a reactive thought in response to trauma - perhaps a way of coping or explaining the unexplainable - solidifies over time into a belief that defines the way survivors see themselves. This belief system is often characterized by feelings of unworthiness, guilt, shame, and helplessness. Instead of recognizing that something terrible happened to them, survivors come to believe that they are the source of their suffering - that they are fundamentally flawed, and this is why they were hurt.

As these beliefs deepen, trauma becomes the filter through which survivors view the world. Relationships that once seemed safe and nurturing are now tinged with suspicion and fear. Survivors may find themselves withdrawing from loved ones, doubting their intentions, or fearing further betrayal. Opportunities that might once have been seen as exciting are overshadowed by self-doubt. "I'm not good enough" or "I don't deserve this" become the internal responses to new possibilities. Life becomes a daily battle, not only against the external world but against the internal dialogue that trauma has created.

This is the most destructive aspect of trauma - it doesn't stay contained to the event. It infiltrates every corner of a person's life, shaping their thoughts, emotions, relationships, and sense of self. It creates an ever-present undercurrent of anxiety, fear, and shame that can be difficult to identify and even harder to challenge. Many survivors don't even realize that they are living within a narrative created by their trauma. They've been living with these thoughts and beliefs for so long that they feel like part of their identity, not something that can be changed.

And this is where many traditional therapeutic approaches fall short. In the focus on revisiting and processing the traumatic event itself, there is often little attention paid to the ongoing narratives the trauma has created. While understanding the trauma is crucial, it is not enough. Survivors need more than just intellectual insight - they need tools to challenge the distorted beliefs that have taken root in their minds.

This is where the R.E.S.T. Method becomes so crucial. Unlike many traditional approaches, which primarily seek to understand and process the trauma event itself, the R.E.S.T. Method turns the focus inward - on the narrative that trauma has created and on the ways in which survivors can take control of that narrative. The R.E.S.T. Method doesn't just focus on revisiting what happened; it focuses on rewriting the story that survivors tell themselves about who they are because of what happened.

Revisiting Trauma vs. Rewriting the Narrative

Traditional methods of trauma recovery, such as talk therapy, exposure therapy, or cognitive behavioral approaches, often focus on revisiting the traumatic event. These methods aim to bring understanding, closure, and a sense of mastery over what happened. In many cases, the therapeutic process involves discussing the trauma in detail, identifying the emotions and thoughts associated with it, and processing the pain in a supportive, safe environment. While this approach can be helpful in demystifying trauma and enabling individuals to confront their memories, it often falls short in addressing the most damaging and long-lasting impacts of trauma: the internalized beliefs and harmful narratives that it leaves behind.

Revisiting trauma might allow a person to intellectually understand what happened, providing insight into the circumstances, the behaviors involved, and the reasons why the event was so painful. However, understanding alone doesn't always dismantle the deep emotional residue left by trauma, nor does it necessarily disrupt the damaging beliefs survivors may have adopted about themselves. Trauma is not simply an event; it is an experience that shapes how individuals see the world and themselves long after the event has passed. While traditional methods provide a necessary first step in the healing process, they often fail to address how trauma rewires the brain, alters the emotional landscape, and, most significantly, creates entrenched cognitive distortions about one's identity and safety.

The Emotional Residue of Trauma: The Missing Link

In my work with individuals affected by trauma, I have witnessed this shortcoming countless times - individuals who have gone through years of therapy, who can recount their trauma in painstaking detail, who have examined every nuance of their experience, and yet still feel trapped by it. Their trauma is no longer a mystery to them. They've been through the process of revisiting the event, of dissecting it, and of analyzing every emotional, cognitive, and situational aspect of it. And yet, despite this deep understanding, they remain entangled in the emotional residue that trauma has left behind. Their healing has plateaued because, while they have intellectually processed the trauma, they haven't reshaped how it has influenced their self-concept or their worldview.

Here's the key issue: revisiting trauma can help to explain the "what" and the "why" of trauma, but it doesn't always address the "how." How has trauma reshaped the survivor's self-worth? How has it warped their sense of control or agency? How has it distorted their ability to trust others, experience joy, or feel safe in the world? Survivors may intellectually know what happened to them, and they may have processed the event to some degree, but the narratives that trauma creates - "I am not enough," "I will never be safe," "I am broken" - remain deeply ingrained. These beliefs act as barriers, preventing individuals from moving forward even after they've explored their trauma in therapy.

This gap in traditional trauma recovery approaches is where survivors often feel frustrated and stuck. Despite understanding the trauma and identifying its impacts, they continue to feel as though they are at its mercy. The destructive internal dialogue remains unchecked, keeping them trapped in cycles of self-doubt, fear, and shame. This is because revisiting the trauma doesn't automatically dismantle the harmful beliefs that have formed as a result of it. Trauma has a way of infiltrating a person's identity, telling them they are weak, powerless, or unworthy. Without addressing these internalized narratives, the survivor may continue to struggle with the emotional scars left by the trauma, even if they have intellectually processed the event.

Offering a Different Emphasis: The R.E.S.T. Method's Focus on Rewriting the Narrative

This is where the R.E.S.T. Method offers a different emphasis. Unlike traditional therapeutic methods that primarily focus on revisiting the traumatic event itself, the R.E.S.T. Method shifts attention to what happens after the trauma - the internalized beliefs, the harmful narratives, and the emotional scars that continue to affect the survivor's daily life. Rather than revisiting the trauma repeatedly in hopes of finding new insights, the R.E.S.T. Method provides survivors with a new path forward: the opportunity to rewrite the narrative that trauma has created. It offers a structured way to challenge the distorted beliefs and internal dialogue that keep survivors stuck, empowering them to reclaim their stories and, ultimately, their lives.

The R.E.S.T. Method doesn't ignore the importance of understanding the trauma itself. It recognizes that for many survivors, gaining insight into the "what" and the "why" of their trauma is an essential step toward healing. However, the model goes a step further by addressing the deeper layers of trauma's impact - the layers that deal with how survivors see themselves, how they relate to others, and how they navigate the world moving forward. By focusing on reshaping the narrative of trauma, the R.E.S.T. Method helps survivors not only process their pain but also rewrite the distorted beliefs that have taken root in the wake of trauma.

Rewriting the narrative means transforming the internal dialogue from one of self-blame, fear, and helplessness into a narrative of resilience, strength, and empowerment. Survivors are no longer seen as passive victims of their trauma; instead, they are encouraged to become active participants in their own recovery, taking ownership of the story they tell themselves. The R.E.S.T. Method provides survivors with the tools to challenge the cognitive distortions that trauma creates. It empowers them to dismantle the harmful beliefs that have taken hold and to build a new narrative - one that reflects their resilience, their capacity for healing, and their potential for growth.

The Role of Cognitive Reframing in Rewriting the Narrative

One of the core elements of the R.E.S.T. Method is cognitive reframing. This technique plays a critical role in helping survivors rewrite the narrative of their trauma by challenging the harmful thoughts and beliefs that trauma has ingrained. Cognitive reframing involves identifying the negative, distorted thoughts that are keeping survivors stuck in patterns of self-doubt, fear, and shame, and replacing them with healthier, more empowering beliefs.

For example, a survivor who has internalized the belief "I am broken because of what happened to me" might, through cognitive reframing, begin to shift that belief to "I am strong because I survived what happened to me." This shift may seem subtle, but it has profound effects on the survivor's emotional and psychological well-being. It allows them to reclaim their sense of self and to begin seeing themselves not as defined by their trauma but as capable of rising above it.

Cognitive reframing is about more than just changing a few thoughts - it's about reshaping the entire internal narrative that a survivor has developed in response to their trauma. It's about shifting the focus from what the trauma took away to what the survivor has gained through their resilience, strength, and perseverance. The R.E.S.T. Method helps survivors recognize that, while they may have been shaped by their trauma, they are not defined by it. They are not victims; they are survivors, and they have the power to take control of their future.

Empowerment Through the R.E.S.T. Method

One of the strengths of the R.E.S.T. Method is its focus on empowerment. Trauma often leaves survivors feeling powerless and out of control, as though their lives have been taken out of their hands. The R.E.S.T. Method gives that control back. It helps survivors understand that, while they may not have had control over what happened to them, they do have control over how they respond to it and how they choose to move forward.

By offering survivors the tools to actively rewrite their internal narrative, the R.E.S.T. Method empowers them to reclaim their sense of agency. It teaches them that healing is not about passively revisiting the trauma or waiting for the pain to fade. Healing is about taking an active role in the process, challenging the distortions that trauma has created, and building a new story - one that reflects resilience, strength, and hope.

Survivors are given the opportunity to move beyond their trauma, to move from a place of victimhood to a place of empowerment, and to create a future that is not defined by the pain of their past but by the strength they have developed through their healing journey. The R.E.S.T. Method offers a new way forward - a way that goes beyond revisiting trauma and instead focuses on rewriting the narrative, reclaiming power, and building a life that is defined by growth, resilience, and possibility.

This is where the R.E.S.T. Method offers a different emphasis. Rather than solely focusing on the traumatic event, the model shifts attention to the aftermath of trauma - the internalized beliefs, the harmful narratives, and the emotional scars that continue to affect the survivor's daily life. The R.E.S.T. Method provides a pathway to not only process trauma but to actively rewrite the narrative that surrounds it. Survivors are given the tools to challenge the distortions that trauma creates, and to reclaim their story from a place of empowerment.

Release: Letting Go of Trauma's Emotional Grip

The first stage of the R.E.S.T. Method is Release, a crucial step in helping trauma survivors create emotional distance from the overwhelming feelings their trauma generates. Trauma often leaves individuals feeling as though they are trapped in a whirlwind of emotions - fear, anger, shame, and sadness swirling around them uncontrollably. The emotional intensity can be so overpowering that it becomes difficult to see beyond the pain. In many cases, trauma survivors feel as though they are at the mercy of their emotions, powerless to control the waves of distress that wash over them.

The Release phase is about helping survivors recognize that while their emotions are real and valid, they do not have to be all-consuming. Through techniques like mindfulness, grounding exercises, and emotional regulation, survivors learn to observe their emotions without being overwhelmed by them. They begin to understand that while emotions may rise and fall like waves, they are not permanent. By cultivating a sense of emotional distance, survivors can start to regain control over their emotional landscape.

This process is not about suppressing or denying emotions; rather, it is about learning to engage with them in a healthy and constructive way. It's about recognizing that emotions are transient, that they do not define the survivor's entire experience, and that there are tools available to manage them effectively. This is often the first step in reclaiming a sense of agency in the healing process.

For many survivors, the Release phase represents a turning point in their recovery. It is the moment when they realize that they have the power to manage their emotions, rather than being controlled by them.

This realization is incredibly empowering, as it marks the beginning of a shift from passivity to active engagement in the healing process.

Examine Through Time: Challenging the False Permanence of Trauma

One of the most devastating cognitive distortions that trauma creates is the belief that the pain, fear, and distress will last forever. Trauma survivors often feel as though they are trapped in a never-ending loop of suffering, unable to imagine a future where they feel safe or happy again. This sense of permanence can be deeply demoralizing, leading survivors to believe that healing is impossible and that they are doomed to live with the effects of trauma for the rest of their lives.

The Examine Through Time phase of the R.E.S.T. Method is designed to challenge this false sense of permanence. Temporal reframing involves encouraging survivors to view their trauma from the perspective of time, helping them understand that the intense emotions they are experiencing in the present are not permanent. By projecting themselves into the future and imagining a time when the emotional intensity has lessened, survivors can begin to shift their relationship with their trauma.

This phase is about offering survivors hope - a reminder that healing is a gradual process and that with time, the pain will subside. Temporal reframing allows survivors to break free from the cognitive trap that convinces them their current state of suffering is permanent. It helps them see that while the journey to healing may be long and difficult, there is light at the end of the tunnel.

In practice, time-based reframing encourages survivors to visualize their future selves - stronger, more resilient, and more at peace. It helps them imagine a life where trauma no longer dominates their thoughts or controls their emotions. By anchoring their recovery in the possibility of a better future, survivors are given a sense of direction and purpose, which is essential for maintaining hope and motivation during the healing process.

Select What Matters: Letting Go of What Doesn't Matter

Trauma survivors often develop a hypervigilant sense of responsibility, feeling as though they must control every aspect of their lives in order to prevent further harm. This need for control is exhausting and often leads to feelings of frustration and helplessness, as survivors quickly realize that they cannot control everything. The third phase of the R.E.S.T. Method, Select What Matters, teaches survivors to let go of the things they cannot control and to focus their energy on what truly matters.

Selective nihilism is about recognizing that not everything in life is worth the emotional energy we invest in it. It's about discerning what is truly important and releasing the rest. This phase helps survivors break free from the exhausting cycle of trying to manage every possible outcome and teaches them to prioritize their emotional energy toward the things that align with their core values and personal growth.

By letting go of the need to control everything, survivors free themselves from the constant anxiety and hypervigilance that trauma often creates. They begin to understand that they don't have to be responsible for everything, and that it's okay to release the things that don't serve their well-being. This phase is incredibly liberating, as it allows survivors to focus on what truly matters - whether that's their relationships, their passions, or their personal development.

A client I worked with struggled deeply with the belief that they needed to control every aspect of their environment to prevent further trauma. This belief led to constant anxiety and emotional exhaustion, as they tried to manage every detail of their life in an attempt to feel safe. By working through the Select What Matters phase, they were able to let go of the need for control and focus their energy on the aspects of their life that truly brought them fulfillment and joy. This shift in perspective was transformative, allowing them to experience a newfound sense of peace and freedom.

Transform Meaning: Transforming Trauma into Purpose

The final phase of the R.E.S.T. Method, Transform Meaning, is about finding purpose in the pain of trauma. This doesn't mean glorifying the trauma or suggesting that it was necessary, but rather integrating the experience into a larger narrative of growth and personal transformation. Trauma survivors often feel that their suffering is senseless, that it has no meaning or purpose beyond the pain it has caused. However, the process of healing requires survivors to find meaning in their trauma - not to justify it, but to transform it into a source of strength, wisdom, and growth.

Existential meaning involves helping survivors reflect on the lessons they've learned through their trauma and how those lessons can inform their future. It's about recognizing that while the trauma was deeply painful, it has also shaped them into the person they are today. By finding meaning in their suffering, survivors are able to transform their trauma into a source of purpose and resilience.

For many survivors, this phase represents a profound shift in their understanding of themselves and their trauma. Instead of viewing the trauma as something that has diminished them, they begin to see it as something that has shaped their strength and character. The pain of their trauma becomes a source of wisdom and empathy, allowing them to connect with others on a deeper level and to live with a greater sense of purpose.

One individual I worked with, who had experienced profound loss, found that by reflecting on the resilience they had developed in the aftermath of their trauma, they were able to find a renewed sense of purpose. Their trauma had led them to develop deeper empathy for others, to appreciate the fragility of life, and to seek out ways to contribute to their community. By finding meaning in their suffering, they were able to transform their trauma into a source of personal strength and purpose.

Why the R.E.S.T. Method Matters

The R.E.S.T. Method is essential because it moves beyond traditional approaches to trauma recovery, offering survivors a structured, step-by-step process that addresses the cognitive, emotional, and existential layers of trauma. It recognizes that trauma is not just an event - it is an experience that reshapes the way survivors see themselves and the world. Through the R.E.S.T. Method, survivors are empowered to reclaim their narrative, transform their internal dialogue, and rebuild their sense of self.

The model is a structured pathway in trauma recovery because it doesn't just focus on revisiting the trauma - it teaches survivors how to move beyond it. Through each phase of the model, survivors are given the tools to move from survival mode to a life of thriving. They learn to let go of the emotional weight of trauma, challenge the false narratives it creates, and transform their pain into purpose and strength.

In a world where trauma often feels inescapable, the R.E.S.T. Method offers a way forward - a path to healing that honors the pain of the past while empowering survivors to reclaim their future. Trauma survivors deserve more than just the ability to revisit their pain - they deserve the opportunity to move beyond it, transcend the past, and embrace a future defined by growth, resilience, and purpose.

By embracing the R.E.S.T. Method, trauma survivors become active participants in their healing journey. They are no longer passive recipients of therapy or counseling - they are empowered to rewrite their narrative, transform their pain into strength, and build a future filled with possibility. The R.E.S.T. Method can be a valuable guide looking to move beyond survival and into a life of thriving.

The R.E.S.T. Method offers a structured way to look beyond merely understanding and processing the traumatic event, but rather, fully reclaiming the survivor's power to rewrite their narrative and reclaim their lives. This model reflects a profound evolution in our understanding of trauma and its aftershocks - an acknowledgment that trauma is not just an external event but something that takes deep root within, reshaping how survivors see themselves and the world around them. At its core, the R.E.S.T. Method provides a framework for healing that acknowledges the multifaceted nature of trauma - its cognitive, emotional, and existential dimensions - and empowers survivors to not only confront their pain but to move beyond it.

Traditional approaches to trauma recovery have been invaluable in helping survivors process what happened to them. They've provided safe spaces for revisiting the trauma, dissecting its emotional impact, and gaining intellectual closure. However, these methods have often fallen short in addressing the longer-lasting, subtler impacts of trauma - the ingrained beliefs, the toxic narratives, and the identity-shaping distortions that linger long after the event has been processed. The

R.E.S.T. Method recognizes that trauma doesn't just live in the mind's memory of the event but continues to influence every thought, every relationship, and every decision. For many survivors, revisiting the trauma brings understanding, but understanding alone does not provide the freedom to move forward or the power to reshape the future.

The Complexity of Trauma and the Simplicity of Hope

The R.E.S.T. Method stands apart because it meets trauma survivors where they are, offering a comprehensive yet accessible path to healing. Trauma is inherently complex, and each individual's experience of it is unique. No two journeys are the same, and no two sets of emotional scars are identical. Trauma weaves itself into every aspect of a person's life - it infiltrates their thoughts, reshapes their relationships, and alters their sense of identity. Survivors are often left grappling with a tangled web of emotions: fear, shame, anger, guilt, and sadness. They may feel as if they've lost their sense of self, as if the trauma has consumed their ability to live fully and authentically.

Yet, despite the complexity of trauma, there remains a simplicity in the fundamental need for hope, for a way forward that offers clarity, empowerment, and resilience. This is where the R.E.S.T. Method shines. It offers survivors not just hope but a structured and empowering process through which they can rebuild their lives. Hope, within the R.E.S.T. framework, is not a passive feeling but an active pursuit. It is something survivors create for themselves as they progress through the stages of the model - reclaiming their story, reframing their beliefs, and ultimately rising above their trauma with newfound strength and purpose.

R.E.S.T. Practice

Applying the Introduction

Before moving into the method, notice the story trauma has been telling about you. The purpose of this opening reflection is not to debate whether the pain mattered. It did. The purpose is to begin noticing where the pain became identity, expectation, self-blame, or fear.

Release: What needs to settle before you analyze this?

____

____

____

Examine Through Time: How might this feel or look different with time, distance, and support?

____

____

____

Select What Matters: What truly deserves your energy here?

____

____

____

Transform Meaning: What meaning can be built without minimizing what happened?

____

____

____

Reflection Prompts

- What story has trauma most often told me about myself?

- Where do I notice that story shaping my choices?

- What would it mean to question the story without denying the pain?

Gentle Reminder

Do not force insight before your body has enough safety to hold it. Regulation comes before interpretation. You can return to any exercise slowly, briefly, and with support.

Chapter 1

Understanding Trauma

What is Trauma?

To put it simply, trauma is any experience that overwhelms your ability to cope. It's not just the event itself that causes trauma, but how it leaves you feeling afterward - helpless, unsafe, or powerless. Trauma can strike like a lightning bolt in the middle of an ordinary life, such as a car accident, a natural disaster, or an assault. Or it can creep in slowly, like a tide rising over time - through ongoing emotional abuse, neglect, or even the relentless pressure of chronic stress.

What makes trauma so personal is that no two people experience it in the same way. You and I could go through the exact same event, and yet how we feel about it, how it changes us, might be completely different. That's because trauma is deeply subjective - it's influenced by who we are, how we've lived, what support we have, and even our genetic makeup. It's not the event itself that determines whether something is traumatic; it's how our minds and bodies react to it.

In the moments following a traumatic event, the body's natural defense system kicks in. Your heart pounds, your muscles tighten, and your senses become hyper-aware. This is the fight, flight, or freeze response - your body's way of protecting you in the face of danger. But trauma doesn't always end when the danger passes. Sometimes, your brain and body stay stuck in survival mode. Long after the event is over, you might find yourself still on edge, still feeling like you're in danger, even when you're safe.

Trauma isn't just something that happens to your mind; it's something that happens to your body as well. It's stored in your muscles, your nervous system, your very cells. And that's why healing from trauma often requires more than just "talking it out." It requires understanding how trauma lives inside of you, and learning how to release it, piece by piece, so you can move forward.

Types of Traumas: Acute, Chronic, and Complex

Not all trauma is the same. Trauma comes in many forms, and understanding the differences can help you better understand your own experience.

Acute Trauma: This type of trauma is caused by a single, unexpected event. Picture yourself driving down the highway on a sunny afternoon when suddenly, you're involved in a car accident. That jarring, life-threatening moment can leave you shaken, replaying the event over and over in your mind. Acute trauma is like a sharp, sudden wound - it leaves you reeling, but because it's tied to a specific event, it can sometimes be easier to identify and work through.

Chronic Trauma: Chronic trauma happens when you're exposed to stress over a long period of time. It's the kind of trauma that seeps into your life slowly, like water through a crack in the foundation. It might be the result of living in a volatile household, experiencing ongoing bullying, or enduring a long-term abusive relationship. Over time, the constant stress wears you down, leaving you feeling powerless and trapped.

Complex Trauma: Complex trauma is often the most difficult to understand and heal from. It results from repeated, long-term exposure to traumatic situations, often beginning in childhood. If you grew up in an unsafe or unstable environment, where neglect or abuse was part of your everyday life, you may have experienced complex trauma. This type of trauma impacts the very core of who you are - it shapes your sense of identity, your ability to trust, and how you relate to others.

Each type of trauma leaves its own unique mark, but one thing they all have in common is their ability to make you feel stuck, like you're living in a loop where the past keeps invading the present. Recognizing the type of trauma you've experienced is an important part of beginning your healing journey. It's not just about labeling your experience; it's about understanding it deeply, so you can start to reclaim control over your story.

The Emotional and Physiological Impact of Trauma

When you think of trauma, you might first picture the emotional toll it takes - fear, anxiety, depression, guilt, or shame. These are the feelings that sit heavy in your chest, that keep you up at night, that make you feel like you're carrying a burden too heavy to bear. But trauma doesn't just live in your emotions. It lives in your body, too.

Trauma leaves an imprint on the brain and nervous system, changing the way they function. When you experience a traumatic event, your brain's alarm system - the amygdala - kicks into high gear. It floods your body with stress hormones like adrenaline and cortisol, preparing you to either fight, flee, or freeze. In the moment, this reaction might save your life. But long after the danger has passed, your brain might still be stuck in survival mode.

For many trauma survivors, this means living in a constant state of alert. You might feel on edge all the time, easily startled by loud noises, or find it hard to relax. This heightened state of awareness can take a toll on your body, leading to chronic fatigue, headaches, digestive issues, and even heart problems. Over time, the stress of living in survival mode wears you down, both physically and mentally.

And then there's the emotional side of trauma. Trauma can leave you feeling disconnected from yourself and the world around you. You might struggle with feelings of worthlessness, guilt, or shame - emotions that can be deeply isolating. These emotions often come with a sense of confusion, like you can't quite make sense of why you feel the way you do. That's because trauma impacts the prefrontal cortex, the part of the brain responsible for logical thinking and emotional regulation. This makes it hard to process your emotions or understand why you're reacting the way you are.

You might find yourself stuck in cycles of intrusive thoughts, flashbacks, or nightmares - reliving the trauma as if it's happening all over again. These are not just memories. They are your brain's way of trying to make sense of the trauma, but without the right tools, these intrusive experiences can feel overwhelming.

How Trauma Shapes Our Identity

One of the most insidious aspects of trauma is how it seeps into your sense of self. Trauma doesn't just make you feel scared or sad - it can change how you see yourself entirely. It plants seeds of doubt and insecurity, leading you to question your worth, your capabilities, and even your right to happiness.

For survivors of complex trauma, this shift in identity can be particularly profound. When trauma happens over a long period, especially during childhood, it disrupts the natural development of self-worth and self-identity. You may internalize the belief that you are not deserving of love or that there's something fundamentally wrong with you. These beliefs, though false, can become deeply ingrained, making it hard to imagine a future where you feel whole or worthy.

Trauma also influences how you relate to others. You may struggle to trust people, even those closest to you. It can feel like everyone is a potential threat, and vulnerability becomes something to be avoided at all costs. This leads to emotional walls, making it difficult to form deep, meaningful connections with others. At the same time, trauma can pull you toward unhealthy relationships - seeking out dynamics that mirror the instability or chaos of the trauma itself, reinforcing the belief that safety and love are always out of reach.

But despite how deeply trauma can shape your identity, it doesn't have to be permanent. Healing is possible. By learning to recognize the ways trauma has affected your sense of self, you can start to rewrite the story. Cognitive reframing, which you'll explore later in this book, is one powerful way to begin shifting those harmful beliefs and reclaiming your true identity.

Recognizing Trauma Responses in Daily Life

The thing about trauma is that it doesn't stay in the past. It shows up in the present, often in ways you might not even recognize at first. Trauma responses become woven into the fabric of your daily life, sometimes so subtly that they feel like just another part of who you are.

Perhaps you find yourself avoiding certain places, people, or activities because they remind you of what happened. This is a form of avoidance, one of the most common trauma responses. While it might feel like a way to protect yourself, avoidance can also limit your ability to fully engage with life. Over time, it can make your world smaller, as more and more things become associated with the trauma.

Another common trauma response is hypervigilance. This means constantly scanning your environment for potential threats, even when there's no danger present. You might feel jumpy or easily startled, always on the lookout for signs that something bad is about to happen. Hypervigilance keeps you trapped in survival mode, making it hard to relax or enjoy the moment.

You might also experience emotional numbness. This is your brain's way of protecting you from further pain by shutting down your ability to feel emotions altogether. While this might seem like a relief at first, emotional numbness can leave you feeling disconnected - not just from the pain, but also from joy, excitement, or love.

And then there's self-sabotage - the unconscious ways you undermine your own success, happiness, or relationships. This can happen because trauma has made you believe that you're not worthy of good things, or because vulnerability feels too risky. It's a way of protecting yourself from the possibility of further hurt, even if it means keeping yourself stuck.

Recognizing these trauma responses in your daily life is the first step toward healing. Once you're aware of how trauma is influencing your thoughts, feelings, and behaviors, you can begin to take steps to change them. This book will guide you through the process of challenging and reshaping these responses, helping you reclaim control over your life.

Trauma may have shaped parts of your life, but it does not have to define you. Understanding the depth and breadth of its impact is the first step toward liberation. As we move forward into the R.E.S.T. Method, you'll gain the tools you need to begin rewriting your story. You will discover practical ways to transform your trauma and reclaim your sense of self, moving from survival to resilience, from pain to power. Healing is not just possible - it's within your reach, waiting for you to take the first step.

R.E.S.T. Practice

Applying Understanding Trauma

This chapter helps you name the forms trauma can take and recognize how it may show up in daily life, relationships, identity, and the body.

Release: What needs to settle before you analyze this?

____

____

____

Examine Through Time: How might this feel or look different with time, distance, and support?

____

____

____

Select What Matters: What truly deserves your energy here?

____

____

____

Transform Meaning: What meaning can be built without minimizing what happened?

____

____

____

Reflection Prompts

- Which trauma responses do I recognize in my daily life?

____

____

- Where do I feel survival mode in my body?

____

____

- What kind of support would make healing safer for me?

____

____

Gentle Reminder

Do not force insight before your body has enough safety to hold it. Regulation comes before interpretation. You can return to any exercise slowly, briefly, and with support.

Chapter 2

Cognitive Reframing: Changing the Story Pain Created

What is Cognitive Reframing?

As explored in the introduction, trauma often feels like an immovable weight - a burden that casts a long shadow over our lives, shaping thoughts, emotions, and actions long after the event has passed. It becomes a filter through which we see the world, a dark lens that distorts our reality and keeps us anchored to the pain. For many trauma survivors, this weight becomes an ever-present companion, limiting their ability to move forward or to see themselves and their potential clearly. Traditional therapeutic approaches, while often helpful, may address the immediate emotional wounds but can leave deeper, more persistent scars: cognitive distortions. These are the ingrained patterns of thinking that keep survivors trapped in cycles of fear, guilt, shame, and hopelessness.

This is where cognitive reframing steps in - offering not a way to forget trauma or diminish its impact, but a way to change how we perceive and relate to it. Cognitive reframing doesn't pretend that trauma never happened. Instead, it equips you with the mental tools to reshape your understanding of what the trauma means in your life. By shifting the interpretation of past events, cognitive reframing allows survivors to reclaim control over the narratives they tell themselves. This process doesn't erase trauma but transforms how it is processed and stored in the mind, shifting it from a dominating force into something more manageable, something from which growth and healing can emerge.

The Power of Cognitive Reframing

At its core, cognitive reframing is about changing the meaning you assign to your experiences. Trauma survivors often develop automatic, reflexive thoughts - thoughts rooted in pain, fear, and loss. These thoughts tend to surface quickly and powerfully, becoming self-reinforcing over time. For example, after a traumatic event, a person might automatically think, "I'm never safe," or "I'm not worthy of love," or "I'm to blame for what happened." These automatic thoughts are cognitive distortions that, while they may have some grounding in the trauma, do not reflect the full truth of a survivor's experience or worth.

Cognitive reframing allows you to step outside of these automatic responses. It offers the opportunity to pause and ask, "Is this thought truly serving me? Is it grounded in reality, or is it a product of my trauma?" By questioning the validity of these deeply ingrained beliefs, you begin to loosen their hold on your mind. Cognitive reframing encourages you to shift from a narrative of victimhood or helplessness to one of empowerment and resilience. You begin to realize that while you cannot always control what has happened to you, you can control how you interpret and respond to it.

But cognitive reframing is not just about "thinking positively" or putting a silver lining on your suffering. It's about finding a more nuanced and balanced perspective that honors both the pain of what you have experienced and the possibility for growth and healing. For example, a person who has experienced betrayal might initially believe, "No one can be trusted." This belief, while understandable in the wake of the trauma, is an overgeneralization - a cognitive distortion. Through reframing, that thought might evolve into something more balanced: "Some people have betrayed me, but that doesn't mean everyone will." This shift does not deny the pain of betrayal, but it opens up the possibility of trust, connection, and healing in the future.

Cognitive Reframing as a Practice

Cognitive reframing is not a one-time event - it's a practice. Trauma, especially when it is severe or repeated, carves deep grooves in our thought patterns. The distorted beliefs and automatic thoughts that emerge from trauma become habitual, shaping how we view ourselves, others, and the world. These patterns don't change overnight, but with consistent effort, cognitive reframing becomes a powerful tool for reprogramming the mind. Each time you reframe a distorted thought, you are creating new neural pathways in the brain, weakening the old, trauma-driven patterns and strengthening healthier, more adaptive ways of thinking.

Think of it like rewiring your brain. Trauma can cause your brain to get stuck in a loop - triggering the same emotions, fears, and responses again and again. Cognitive reframing interrupts that loop, offering a way to redirect your thoughts down a different, more productive path. Over time, these new pathways become stronger, while the old, maladaptive ones weaken. This is the essence of neuroplasticity - the brain's ability to reorganize itself and form new connections. Cognitive reframing taps into this natural ability, helping to undo some of the damage trauma has caused and allowing the brain to heal and recover.

Let's consider an example. A person who has experienced childhood neglect might grow up believing, "I'm unlovable." This belief, born from years of emotional deprivation, becomes a core part of their identity. But through cognitive reframing, that individual might begin to ask, "Is it really true that I'm unlovable, or is that just how I was made to feel by circumstances beyond my control?" Over time, that thought can be reshaped into something like, "I didn't receive the love I deserved, but that doesn't mean I'm unworthy of love." This subtle shift in thinking, though it may seem small, can be profoundly healing. It allows the person to open themselves up to love and connection in ways they may not have thought possible.

The Science of Trauma: How It Warps Our Thinking

Trauma is more than just an emotional wound. It reshapes our brain, distorting how we process information, memories, and emotions, and leaving us trapped in patterns of fear and pain. When we experience trauma, its impact extends deep into our neurological systems, fundamentally altering the way our brain functions. This shift creates a persistent imbalance between our survival instincts and our ability to think clearly, manage emotions, and navigate the world with a sense of safety.

At the core of this transformation is the amygdala, the brain's emotional command center. The amygdala's primary role is to detect threats and trigger the fight-or-flight response, a survival mechanism that is essential in life-threatening situations. In moments of danger, this system floods the body with stress hormones like adrenaline and cortisol, preparing us to confront or flee from harm. This heightened state of alertness, designed to keep us alive, allows us to react quickly and instinctively in moments of crisis.

However, trauma hijacks this process. While the fight-or-flight response is crucial in the moment of trauma, the real issue arises after the event has passed. For many trauma survivors, the amygdala remains locked in overdrive long after the threat is gone. It's as though the brain becomes stuck in a loop of hypervigilance, constantly scanning the environment for danger, even in places where no real threat exists. Everyday situations that should feel neutral or even safe can suddenly seem overwhelming, triggering a cascade of anxiety, fear, and emotional distress.

This state of hypervigilance is exhausting. It's like living life with the volume turned up too high - every sound, every movement, every emotion is amplified, making it difficult to relax, concentrate, or feel secure. Survivors often describe feeling like they're "on edge," never able to fully let their guard down. Even in the most benign circumstances, their nervous system remains in perpetual alarm mode, ready to fight, flee, or freeze at a moment's notice. This makes simple tasks, like going to the grocery store or engaging in social interactions, feel daunting and overwhelming. It's as though the trauma creates a filter through which all experiences are processed, coloring even the most mundane aspects of life with a sense of impending threat.

While the amygdala is firing on all cylinders, the prefrontal cortex - the part of the brain responsible for logical thinking, decision-making, and emotional regulation - takes a backseat. In a healthy brain, the prefrontal cortex and the amygdala work together in balance. The prefrontal cortex assesses situations rationally, helping us to think critically, evaluate options, and regulate our emotional responses. But trauma disrupts this balance, weakening the prefrontal cortex's ability to function effectively. Instead of calmly processing emotions and making thoughtful decisions, trauma survivors often feel overwhelmed by emotional reactions that seem disproportionate to the circumstances.

It's as if the brain becomes trapped in survival mode, unable to shift back to a state of calm, reasoned thinking. Everyday situations can evoke the same emotional intensity as the original trauma, leaving survivors feeling as though they're reliving the experience over and over again. The brain has rewired itself to prioritize survival at the expense of peace, clarity, and rational thought.

This shift in the brain's functioning results in cognitive distortions - maladaptive patterns of thinking that are shaped by trauma and skewed by emotions like fear, guilt, or shame. These distortions are not just fleeting thoughts; they are deeply ingrained beliefs that arise as a way for the brain to make sense of the trauma. But rather than aiding in healing, these distorted beliefs often serve to reinforce the trauma, keeping the individual stuck in cycles of pain and suffering.

Take, for example, a common cognitive distortion that emerges after trauma: "I'm always in danger." This belief, while initially rooted in the real experience of threat, becomes generalized over time. It spreads like a shadow over all aspects of life, distorting the individual's perception of safety. The world becomes a place where danger lurks around every corner, leaving the survivor constantly on guard, unable to relax or feel secure. Even in safe situations, the brain remains convinced that harm is just around the corner.

Or consider the equally pervasive distortion, "I'm to blame for what happened." This belief is especially common among survivors of abuse or violence. In an attempt to make sense of the trauma, the brain may turn inward, leading the individual to blame themselves for the event. Over time, this self-blame becomes a prison, trapping the survivor in cycles of guilt and shame. Even when logic suggests otherwise, the belief remains: "It must have been my fault."

These cognitive distortions are not harmless. They shape how trauma survivors view the world and themselves, affecting how they engage with new experiences, relationships, and their own healing process. Left unchallenged, these distorted beliefs deepen emotional wounds, making it difficult to move forward or find peace after trauma. The trauma becomes a filter through which all experiences are interpreted, reinforcing feelings of hopelessness, worthlessness, and perpetual danger.

But here's the good news: while trauma may alter the brain, it does not have to be a permanent sentence. The brain's capacity for neuroplasticity - its ability to reorganize and form new neural connections - offers hope. Neuroplasticity means that the brain can change again, this time in the direction of healing. This is where cognitive reframing comes into play as a powerful intervention.

Challenging Cognitive Distortions

Trauma distorts how we perceive the world, shaping thought patterns that can trap survivors in cycles of negative thinking. Cognitive distortions are exaggerated or irrational patterns of thought that often stem from trauma. These distortions warp reality and create a sense of helplessness, leading survivors to believe that the painful thoughts and feelings created by trauma are facts rather than conditioned responses. One of the most powerful tools for breaking free from these distorted patterns is cognitive reframing, which allows survivors to challenge these harmful beliefs and rewire their thinking.

Cognitive Distortions and How Cognitive Reframing Works

Before delving into how the R.E.S.T. Method addresses these distortions, it's important to understand the primary types of cognitive distortions that often result from trauma. The most common distortions include catastrophizing, overgeneralization, and black-and-white thinking - each of which locks individuals into a limited and self-defeating worldview.

Catastrophizing

Catastrophizing occurs when someone expects the worst possible outcome in every situation. For example, a trauma survivor might think, "If I try to build a relationship again, it will end in betrayal, just like before." This kind of thinking leads to unnecessary anxiety and discourages survivors from taking risks, forming relationships, or stepping outside their comfort zones.

Cognitive reframing challenges this by asking important questions: Is it true that every relationship will end in betrayal? What evidence do I have that supports or contradicts this belief? Are there examples in my life where I've experienced trust or connection? These questions push the survivor to reexamine the belief that betrayal is inevitable. In doing so, they see that, while betrayal has occurred in the past, it is not a guaranteed outcome in the future. Cognitive reframing allows survivors to separate past experiences from future possibilities, fostering a sense of empowerment to engage with life more fully and take positive risks.

Overgeneralization

Overgeneralization is a cognitive distortion that occurs when someone takes a single negative event and applies it broadly across all aspects of their life. For instance, after experiencing one failure, a person might internalize the belief, "I fail at everything I do." This type of thinking is deeply disempowering, as it paints life in broad strokes that are overly pessimistic and untrue.

Cognitive reframing helps individuals challenge this by asking, Is it true that I fail at everything, or were there specific circumstances where I struggled? Can I think of instances where I succeeded or showed resilience? By focusing on the nuance of their experiences, survivors can start to see that they are capable of success and that failure, though painful, is not all-encompassing. This creates a more balanced narrative, where mistakes are seen as opportunities for growth rather than a reflection of one's overall worth or abilities.

Black-and-White Thinking

Black-and-white thinking - also known as all-or-nothing thinking - is the tendency to see situations in extreme terms. For trauma survivors, this often manifests as, "If I'm not perfect, I'm a failure," or, "If I'm not completely safe, I'm in constant danger." This rigid way of thinking makes it difficult to see the complexities and nuances of life, leaving survivors feeling stuck in polarized, absolute terms.

Cognitive reframing encourages flexibility by challenging these all-or-nothing thoughts: Is it true that I have to be perfect to be successful? Are there situations where I wasn't perfect but still did well? This shift allows individuals to recognize that mistakes or imperfections don't define their overall success or safety. It fosters a more compassionate and realistic view of oneself, where both strengths and weaknesses coexist, and mistakes are not the end but part of the journey.

The R.E.S.T. Method: Addressing Cognitive Distortions at Every Stage

While cognitive reframing is a powerful tool on its own, the R.E.S.T. Method offers a structured, multi-faceted approach that deepens and broadens the impact of reframing. The model works as a funnel, guiding survivors through various stages of healing and allowing them to filter out the noise of distorted beliefs, outdated emotional responses, and lingering trauma. Each stage of R.E.S.T. - Release, Examine Through Time, Select What Matters, and Transform Meaning - builds upon cognitive reframing, addressing distortions in a layered, comprehensive manner.

The first stage of the R.E.S.T. model, Release, is about letting go of the initial emotional charge associated with trauma. When survivors are overwhelmed with intense emotions, it becomes difficult to think clearly or process thoughts rationally. Cognitive distortions, such as catastrophizing, often arise when emotions are heightened. In this stage, survivors are encouraged to use grounding techniques and mindfulness practices to release some of that emotional intensity, creating space for reframing to occur.

For example, by practicing deep breathing or engaging in physical grounding exercises, individuals can begin to calm the amygdala - the brain's emotional center - and activate the prefrontal cortex, which is responsible for rational thought. Once this emotional fog begins to clear, survivors can more effectively challenge their cognitive distortions and reframe their experiences with a clearer, more balanced perspective.

Examine Through Time

The second stage, Examine Through Time, directly addresses cognitive distortions related to time - particularly the belief that one's current pain or trauma-related thoughts are permanent. Catastrophizing and overgeneralization often come with a sense of permanence, such as, "I will always feel this way," or "My failures define my future."

Temporal reframing helps survivors put their current struggles into a broader context.

By visualizing the future and reminding themselves that time changes perspective, survivors can begin to weaken the hold of their cognitive distortions. Implementing time-based reframing encourages the question, "How will I feel about this a year from now? Can I remember a time when something painful eventually felt less intense?" This process of seeing the current moment as part of a larger arc helps to ease the anxiety that comes with black-and-white thinking and catastrophic beliefs.

Select What Matters, the third stage, focuses on filtering out unnecessary emotional investments. Cognitive distortions often lead trauma survivors to invest heavily in areas that don't truly serve their well-being - like overgeneralizing failures or clinging to the fear that catastrophe is imminent. Select What Matters helps survivors ask themselves, "Does this thought or belief really deserve my energy? What aspects of this situation matter most to my core values?"

For example, a survivor who constantly feels overwhelmed by the need to be perfect may begin to question whether perfectionism is truly necessary for their happiness or growth. By letting go of the need for perfection, they reclaim emotional freedom and refocus on what truly matters, such as building meaningful relationships or pursuing personal fulfillment.

Finally, the R.E.S.T. model concludes with Transform Meaning - a stage that moves beyond reframing individual thoughts and instead asks survivors to find deeper purpose in their experiences. While cognitive reframing addresses specific distortions, Transform Meaning invites survivors to view their trauma through a wider lens of personal growth. Rather than seeing trauma as something that permanently diminishes them, survivors are encouraged to reflect on how their experiences have deepened their empathy, resilience, or understanding of life's complexities.

In this stage, overgeneralization or black-and-white thinking can be challenged by asking, "What has this experience taught me about who I am? How has my trauma allowed me to grow, even in painful ways?"

Finding meaning in suffering doesn't erase the trauma, but it transforms the way survivors relate to it. It becomes part of their larger narrative - a narrative defined by growth, strength, and a deeper connection to themselves and the world.

The R.E.S.T. Method

As we close the chapter on Cognitive Reframing, we've begun to understand how challenging and reshaping distorted thoughts is a critical first step in trauma recovery. Cognitive reframing allows us to shift from a place of helplessness to one of empowerment, where our trauma no longer defines our future. Yet, while reframing individual thoughts is a powerful tool, true healing requires more than just isolated moments of insight. It requires a comprehensive framework that addresses not only the mind but also the emotional and existential wounds trauma leaves behind.

This is where the R.E.S.T. Method comes in - a structured approach that builds on cognitive reframing by guiding survivors through the complexities of emotional release, perspective on time, reallocation of emotional energy, and the search for meaning. In Chapter 2, we will explore how each phase of R.E.S.T. - Release, Examine Through Time, Select What Matters, and Transform Meaning - provides a clear path for integrating these insights into your life. It's a model designed to help you not just survive but thrive in the aftermath of trauma, transforming pain into personal growth.

Now, let's explore the R.E.S.T. Method, breaking down each of its phases to see how they can guide you from a state of emotional overwhelm to a place of resilience and renewed purpose. The next chapter will introduce this practical roadmap, offering a deeper understanding of how the stages of R.E.S.T. work together to foster long-term healing and transformation.

R.E.S.T. Practice

Applying Cognitive Reframing: Changing the Story Pain Created

This chapter helps you identify trauma-shaped thoughts and begin testing them with compassion, evidence, and perspective.

Release: What needs to settle before you analyze this?

____

____

____

Examine Through Time: How might this feel or look different with time, distance, and support?

____

____

____

Select What Matters: What truly deserves your energy here?

____

____

____

Transform Meaning: What meaning can be built without minimizing what happened?

____

____

____

Reflection Prompts

- What thought feels true mainly because it has been repeated for so long?

____

____

- What evidence challenges the trauma-shaped belief?

____

____

- What would a more balanced version of this thought sound like?

____

____

Gentle Reminder

Do not force insight before your body has enough safety to hold it. Regulation comes before interpretation. You can return to any exercise slowly, briefly, and with support.

Chapter 3

The R.E.S.T. Method

The R.E.S.T. Approach to Trauma Recovery

Trauma can fundamentally alter the trajectory of our lives. It can shatter our sense of safety, disrupt our identity, and leave us grappling with the basic meaning of existence. Whether through a sudden accident, the loss of a loved one, a devastating breakup, or a betrayal, trauma leaves deep emotional, psychological, and even physical scars. These wounds are not just momentary; they linger long after the traumatic event itself, embedding themselves into the mind, body, and soul. Trauma becomes like a fog that clouds our future, distorts our present, and traps us in the pain of our past.

However, while trauma is undeniably painful and overwhelming, it does not have to define you. You are not your trauma, and you have the power to reclaim your life, heal, and grow beyond the suffering that once seemed insurmountable. The R.E.S.T. approach is a holistic and structured method designed to not only help you navigate the emotional chaos that trauma brings but to transform that pain into an empowering force for personal growth. R.E.S.T. stands for Release, Examine Through Time, Select What Matters, and Transform Meaning - four foundational pillars that work in tandem to provide a comprehensive, step-by-step framework for trauma recovery. This model guides survivors through the emotional, cognitive, and existential challenges that trauma presents.

The R.E.S.T. approach acknowledges that healing from trauma is not a straightforward journey. Recovery is complex, unpredictable, and filled with emotional highs and lows. In the aftermath of trauma, many of us are left wondering if we will ever feel "normal" again, if we will ever regain the joy, peace, and sense of stability we once had. The R.E.S.T. framework recognizes that recovery isn't about going back to who you were before the trauma - it's about becoming someone stronger, more resilient, and capable of turning pain into growth. This method offers more than just coping mechanisms; it provides a roadmap for building resilience, helping you rise to new levels of empowerment, purpose, and personal strength.

In this book, you will explore each phase of R.E.S.T. in depth. You'll learn how to release the immediate emotional weight of trauma, reframe your perspective on time and healing, focus your emotional energy on what truly matters, and ultimately find meaning in your experiences. The R.E.S.T. approach is designed to help you not only recover from trauma but thrive in the wake of it, turning your pain into a wellspring of power and purpose.

The Emotional and Existential Crisis of Trauma

Trauma does not just affect your emotions - it shakes the very foundation of who you are and how you perceive the world. Trauma isn't simply an emotional wound; it's a profound disruption that touches every aspect of your being. It can make you feel untethered, as though the very ground beneath you has given way, leaving you free-falling into a void of uncertainty and pain. This emotional and existential upheaval is why trauma is so disorienting. It affects not only how you feel but how you see yourself, others, and the world at large.

When a traumatic event occurs, everything you thought you knew about life - your relationships, your sense of control, your ability to trust - may suddenly feel fragile or even irrelevant. Trauma shakes these core aspects of our existence, leaving us questioning not just our emotions but the very essence of who we are. These questions are not merely reflections of emotional pain; they are profound existential dilemmas. Trauma forces you to ask: Why did this happen? How could I have prevented it? How can I ever trust again? What is the point of all this?

In this way, trauma doesn't just disturb your emotional equilibrium; it strikes at the heart of your identity. It challenges the beliefs and assumptions that gave your life structure, meaning, and security. Trauma has the power to turn your world upside down, leaving you in an existential crisis where everything you once believed in - about yourself, others, and the world - feels like it's been called into question.

This disruption is often likened to an earthquake, one that shakes the very core of your being. The emotional impact is like aftershocks that reverberate long after the initial event. Trauma exposes vulnerabilities and forces you to confront beliefs that once seemed solid but now feel fragile or irrelevant. You might find yourself asking whether the values you once held are still applicable. Is love real? Can I ever be safe again? Will my life ever regain its purpose? These are not just fleeting thoughts but deep, existential questions that trauma survivors often grapple with, and the uncertainty they bring can be just as painful as the trauma itself.

The Existential Impact of Trauma

Beyond the immediate emotional devastation, trauma disrupts your sense of meaning and purpose in life. It stirs profound existential questions about the nature of suffering, the fragility of life, and your place in the world. These existential crises are deeply unsettling because they don't just challenge your emotions - they challenge your worldview. Trauma makes you question the very point of existence: Why should I keep going? What is the meaning of all this pain?

These big, universal questions can be overwhelming, and they often leave trauma survivors feeling isolated. You may feel as though no one else can truly understand the depth of your suffering, that the pain you carry sets you apart from others who seem to live untouched by such experiences. This sense of isolation compounds the emotional pain, creating a cycle where the existential questions raised by trauma exacerbate the feelings of despair.

The existential questioning that follows trauma is a natural response to the profound disruption it brings. Trauma destabilizes your entire understanding of yourself and the world. It forces you to reevaluate everything you once believed to be true about your life and the people in it. In the wake of trauma, you may find yourself grappling with feelings of powerlessness, disconnection, and a loss of trust - not only in others but in the world as a whole. Trauma can feel like a betrayal of the very things that once gave your life meaning, leaving you adrift, searching for a new way to understand yourself and the world around you.

Without a clear sense of why the trauma happened or how it fits into the broader context of your life, it can become difficult to envision a future where healing is possible. This lack of meaning can feel suffocating, trapping you in the trauma and making it hard to see a way forward. In this state, it may feel as though the trauma defines you, as though it is the only thing that matters or the only lens through which you can view your life.

Trauma's Assault on Identity

At the heart of trauma's existential crisis is its assault on your sense of identity. Traumatic events often bring a sudden and violent disruption to how you see yourself and your place in the world. Whether the trauma comes from betrayal, loss, violence, or another devastating event, it forces you to confront a version of yourself that feels fragile, broken, and unrecognizable. You may no longer feel like the person you were before the trauma, and your identity, once solid, now feels fractured.

The relationships you relied on may feel alien. The future you once envisioned may seem out of reach. The trust you placed in yourself and others may feel naive or foolish. Trauma distorts these fundamental aspects of your identity, and in its wake, you may feel disconnected from your former self, unsure of who you are now or how to rebuild your sense of self.

This identity crisis often leads to feelings of shame, guilt, and self-blame. Trauma survivors frequently internalize their experiences, believing that they are somehow to blame for what happened, or that they were weak for not preventing it. These feelings can become deeply entrenched, compounding the emotional pain with a distorted sense of self-worth. The person you once thought you were may feel irreparably broken, and the path to rediscovering or rebuilding that person can seem unclear.

Why R.E.S.T. Is Different

The R.E.S.T. approach stands out because it doesn't just address the surface-level symptoms of trauma - it digs into the deeper, more complex ways trauma disrupts your entire sense of self and purpose.

Many traditional trauma recovery methods focus on managing immediate symptoms like anxiety, depression, or PTSD. While these methods are valuable, they often overlook the existential crisis trauma creates. Trauma isn't just an emotional wound; it's an assault on your identity, worldview, and the meaning you once found in life. R.E.S.T. is designed to engage with these deeper issues, offering a comprehensive framework that moves beyond mere coping mechanisms to foster true healing and transformation.

The strength of the R.E.S.T. model lies in its multi-dimensional approach. Trauma changes the way you think, feel, and perceive the world, often distorting your beliefs about yourself and others. R.E.S.T. works to correct these distortions through a structured yet flexible process. It provides the tools to manage overwhelming emotions, reshape distorted thinking, and rebuild a sense of meaning and purpose. Importantly, the framework is not rigid - it's adaptable to your unique experience. This flexibility allows you to move through recovery at your own pace, focusing on the areas where you need the most support.

What truly sets R.E.S.T. apart is its recognition that trauma recovery is not about returning to your old self. Rather, it's about becoming someone stronger and wiser, using your pain as a catalyst for personal growth. The model doesn't offer a quick fix, but instead guides you through a process of self-discovery and empowerment. It addresses the full spectrum of trauma's impact - emotional, cognitive, and existential - allowing you to integrate the trauma into a broader narrative of who you are and where your life is headed.

The Science Behind the R.E.S.T. Method

The R.E.S.T. approach is not merely a set of abstract ideas or a theoretical framework for trauma recovery. It is deeply rooted in the latest findings from neuroscience, particularly the brain's extraordinary ability to change, heal, and adapt through a process known as neuroplasticity. Neuroplasticity refers to the brain's ability to reorganize itself by forming new neural connections in response to experiences, learning, and even emotional healing. This concept is vital because it underscores a hopeful and powerful truth: trauma, while it significantly alters brain function, does not have to cause permanent damage. The brain can be retrained, and the R.E.S.T. model is designed to harness this capacity for positive change.

Trauma's Effect on the Brain: The Amygdala and Prefrontal Cortex

When we experience trauma, it sets off a cascade of physiological and neurological changes, many of which are designed to protect us in the immediate moment but can cause lasting harm if left unchecked. The brain's amygdala, the almond-shaped region responsible for processing emotions and detecting threats, plays a crucial role in triggering the fight-or-flight response. During a traumatic event, the amygdala kicks into high gear, sending signals to the rest of the brain and body to prepare for danger. It releases stress hormones like cortisol and adrenaline, heightening your awareness and preparing you for survival.

This response is critical in life-threatening situations. However, after the trauma has passed, the brain often remains stuck in survival mode. The amygdala, instead of returning to a calm baseline, stays hyperactive - constantly scanning the environment for potential threats, even when none are present. This ongoing hyperactivity leaves trauma survivors in a persistent state of heightened alertness, anxiety, and emotional reactivity. Everyday situations can suddenly seem threatening, and the body reacts as though it is still in danger. This contributes to symptoms of hypervigilance, panic, and emotional dysregulation, making it difficult to feel safe or at ease.

While the amygdala is in overdrive, trauma simultaneously dampens the activity of the prefrontal cortex, the part of the brain responsible for rational thinking, decision-making, and emotional regulation. The prefrontal cortex is like the brain's executive function - allowing you to process information logically, make considered decisions, and regulate your emotions in response to situations. In a healthy, balanced brain, the prefrontal cortex and amygdala work in harmony. The amygdala detects potential threats, and the prefrontal cortex evaluates those threats logically, helping to modulate emotional responses appropriately.

However, trauma disrupts this balance. The overactive amygdala overwhelms the prefrontal cortex, leading to diminished cognitive functioning. This leaves survivors feeling emotionally overwhelmed, reactive, and unable to think clearly. Instead of being able to rationally assess situations and regulate emotions, trauma survivors often feel trapped in emotional loops - experiencing extreme reactions to otherwise neutral situations. This imbalance in brain function also contributes to cognitive distortions - irrational or exaggerated thought patterns that can make trauma feel even more inescapable. These include catastrophizing (expecting the worst to happen), overgeneralization (believing one negative event means all future events will be negative), and black-and-white thinking (seeing situations in absolutes without nuance).

The Role of Neuroplasticity in Healing

The good news is that the brain's ability to reorganize itself through neuroplasticity means that these changes in brain function caused by trauma are not set in stone. Just as trauma reshapes the brain in negative ways, healing experiences can reshape it in positive ways. Neuroplasticity allows the brain to form new neural pathways, essentially rewiring itself in response to new behaviors, thoughts, and emotional processing.

This is where the R.E.S.T. model becomes transformative. By guiding trauma survivors through specific, structured phases of recovery, the model helps to calm the overactive amygdala and engage the prefrontal cortex, thereby restoring balance between these two critical brain regions. Each phase of the R.E.S.T. model is designed to work with the brain's natural capacity for neuroplasticity, encouraging new patterns of thinking, emotional regulation, and personal growth.

Cognitive Reframing: Engaging Neuroplasticity

A central element of the R.E.S.T. model is cognitive reframing, a technique that helps trauma survivors challenge their cognitive distortions and replace them with more balanced, realistic perspectives. This process directly engages the prefrontal cortex, which is essential for logical reasoning and decision-making. When we engage in cognitive reframing, we are essentially training the brain to move away from the automatic, trauma-driven thought patterns that keep us stuck in cycles of pain.

For example, a trauma survivor who has developed the belief, "I'm always in danger," is experiencing a cognitive distortion rooted in the overactive amygdala's constant scanning for threats. Through cognitive reframing, the survivor might ask themselves, Is it true that I'm in danger right now? What evidence do I have to support this belief? Are there examples in my life where I have been safe? By questioning the validity of the distorted thought, the prefrontal cortex is activated to assess the situation more rationally. Over time, the repeated practice of reframing these thoughts helps to weaken the neural pathways associated with trauma-driven beliefs and strengthen new, healthier pathways that are grounded in a more balanced reality.

This rewiring of the brain is not instantaneous - it requires practice, patience, and consistency. However, each time a distorted thought is successfully reframed, the brain is laying down new neural pathways that support emotional regulation and resilience. In this way, cognitive reframing is not just about changing thoughts; it is about rewiring the brain itself, creating a more adaptable, resilient mental framework for navigating future challenges.

The Healing Power of Each Phase of R.E.S.T.

Each phase of the R.E.S.T. model is designed to help the brain heal from the effects of trauma by working with the principles of neuroplasticity and cognitive reframing. Let's break down how each phase contributes to neurological recovery:

Release: The Release phase focuses on helping trauma survivors let go of the immediate emotional charge associated with their trauma. When the brain is overwhelmed by emotional intensity, it becomes difficult to think clearly or rationally. Grounding techniques and mindfulness practices, both of which are core to this phase, help to calm the amygdala and reduce the flow of stress hormones like cortisol. By practicing emotional regulation techniques, survivors learn to deactivate the fight-or-flight response, giving the brain a chance to shift out of survival mode and into a state more conducive to healing.

Examine Through Time: Temporal reframing is a cognitive technique that helps trauma survivors reframe their current pain in the context of time. Trauma can trap the brain in an endless present of suffering, where it feels as though the emotional wounds will never heal. Temporal reframing helps survivors recognize that their current emotional state is temporary, allowing the prefrontal cortex to envision a future where healing has taken place. This shift in perspective reduces the amygdala's grip on the present moment and gives the brain the space to imagine recovery as a real possibility.

Select What Matters: Trauma often leaves survivors emotionally exhausted, pouring energy into areas that don't truly serve their healing. Select What Matters helps survivors filter out unnecessary emotional investments, teaching them to prioritize what matters most. By letting go of non-essential worries and emotional burdens, survivors create cognitive space for healing. This phase is particularly effective at calming the brain's hypervigilance, reducing the constant scanning for threats that the amygdala perpetuates. By focusing on what truly matters, the brain can begin to relax, conserving energy for meaningful pursuits.

Transform Meaning: Logotherapy, which underpins the Transform Meaning phase, is a therapeutic approach that emphasizes finding meaning in suffering. Trauma often leads to a crisis of meaning, where survivors question their purpose and the point of their suffering. By reflecting on how trauma has shaped their understanding of themselves and the world, survivors are encouraged to reframe their pain in a way that allows for personal growth. This process engages both the amygdala and the prefrontal cortex, helping survivors to integrate the trauma into a meaningful narrative rather than being overwhelmed by it.

Why R.E.S.T. Works: A Neuroscientific Perspective

The R.E.S.T. model is effective because it takes into account the way trauma impacts the brain and how healing must be a multi-faceted, integrated process. Trauma recovery requires more than just symptom management; it involves addressing the root of the neurological changes caused by trauma. By working with the brain's neuroplasticity, the R.E.S.T. model helps survivors retrain their brains, restoring emotional regulation, cognitive clarity, and a renewed sense of purpose.

The beauty of neuroplasticity is that it is a lifelong capacity - our brains continue to change and adapt well into adulthood. This means that even if trauma has altered the way you think, feel, and process the world, you can still reclaim control over your brain's functioning. The R.E.S.T. model provides the structure, tools, and techniques to guide this healing process, allowing you to not only recover but thrive.

Through this structured process, the R.E.S.T. model supports long-term resilience, helping survivors develop the cognitive and emotional tools they need to navigate future challenges with strength, clarity, and grace.

Moving Beyond Symptom Management

Many trauma recovery methods focus primarily on symptom management - helping survivors cope with the immediate and painful aftereffects of trauma, such as anxiety, depression, or PTSD. While these interventions are undeniably important, they often leave unaddressed the deeper, existential wounds that trauma inflicts. Trauma doesn't just disrupt your emotional state - it forces you to confront profound questions about your identity, worldview, and sense of purpose. It shakes the very core of who you are and what you believe about the world.

Without addressing these fundamental shifts, survivors may still feel disconnected, lost, or empty even as the more acute symptoms of trauma begin to subside. This is where traditional methods often fall short - they manage the external manifestations of trauma but don't dig deeply enough into the internal reshaping that trauma demands.

R.E.S.T. fills this critical gap by guiding survivors beyond immediate symptom relief and into a process of existential healing. It encourages you to look beyond the surface-level pain and confusion, helping you explore how trauma has reshaped your understanding of yourself and the world around you. Through the structured stages of Release, Time-Based Reframing, Select What Matters, and Transform

Meaning, R.E.S.T. allows you to integrate your trauma into a new, more meaningful narrative of your life - one that acknowledges your suffering while also highlighting your growth, strength, and resilience.

This process is not only about managing pain, but about transforming it. R.E.S.T. helps you address the existential vacuum trauma can create, filling it with a new sense of purpose, connection, and direction. In this way, the framework supports long-term resilience by ensuring that you don't just "get through" trauma but use it as a catalyst for becoming more fully yourself. Healing, in the R.E.S.T. framework, is not about returning to who you were before the trauma - it's about becoming the person you are meant to be because of it.

Transforming Trauma Through Neuroscience

The R.E.S.T. model is not just a collection of therapeutic techniques - it is deeply grounded in the science of how trauma affects the brain and how the brain can heal and adapt through neuroplasticity. Trauma fundamentally alters the brain's structure and function, particularly impacting key areas like the amygdala, which is responsible for emotional processing, and the prefrontal cortex, which governs decision-making, logical thinking, and emotional regulation. These changes are at the root of many trauma-related symptoms, such as emotional dysregulation, hypervigilance, and distorted thinking patterns.

The Role of the Amygdala and Prefrontal Cortex

When trauma occurs, the amygdala, often called the brain's "fear center," becomes hyperactive. Its primary function is to detect threats and trigger the fight-or-flight response, which is crucial for survival in dangerous situations. However, after a traumatic event, the amygdala can remain on high alert long after the danger has passed. This leaves trauma survivors stuck in a state of heightened alertness, where they constantly feel as though they are under threat. The result is often anxiety, panic, hypervigilance, and a chronic sense of emotional dysregulation.

At the same time, trauma weakens the prefrontal cortex, the part of the brain responsible for rational thought, emotional regulation, and decision-making. Under normal circumstances, the prefrontal cortex helps to moderate emotional responses, evaluate risk, and process information logically. But after trauma, its activity diminishes, making it difficult for survivors to think clearly, process their emotions, or make balanced decisions. This diminished function contributes to cognitive distortions, such as catastrophizing, overgeneralization, and black-and-white thinking - all of which reinforce the emotional turmoil caused by trauma.

Rewiring the Brain: How R.E.S.T. Promotes Neuroplasticity

The good news is that the brain is capable of healing itself through a process known as neuroplasticity. Neuroplasticity refers to the brain's ability to reorganize and form new neural connections in response to new experiences, learning, and healing. Just as trauma rewires the brain in negative ways, creating unhealthy patterns of thought and behavior, the R.E.S.T. model helps to rewire the brain in positive ways, fostering resilience, emotional regulation, and healthy cognitive patterns.

One of the key techniques R.E.S.T. employs is cognitive reframing. By helping survivors challenge their cognitive distortions and replace unhealthy beliefs with more balanced perspectives, R.E.S.T. directly engages the brain's capacity for neuroplasticity. Each time a distorted thought - such as "I am always in danger" or "I'm to blame for what happened" - is challenged and reframed, the brain begins to form new neural pathways. These pathways allow the prefrontal cortex to regain its strength, enabling it to once again moderate emotional responses and regulate thought processes.

Over time, this process of reframing helps to quiet the hyperactive amygdala and strengthen the prefrontal cortex. With consistent effort, the brain shifts away from the trauma-driven state of hypervigilance and emotional reactivity, and towards a more balanced state where rational thought and emotional clarity can coexist. The more frequently these new neural pathways are used, the stronger they become. This is how R.E.S.T. harnesses the power of neuroplasticity to promote lasting healing.

Mindfulness and Grounding: Calming the Emotional Storm

Another essential component of the R.E.S.T. model is mindfulness and grounding practices. Mindfulness techniques, which involve bringing focused awareness to the present moment without judgment, help to calm the overactive amygdala and bring the nervous system back to a state of balance. These practices encourage survivors to engage the parasympathetic nervous system, which counteracts the stress response triggered by trauma and promotes a sense of calm and safety.

Grounding exercises, which help individuals reconnect with their bodies and the present moment, further support this process by shifting the brain out of survival mode. When trauma survivors use grounding techniques to focus on sensory experiences - such as the feel of the ground under their feet, or the sound of their own breathing - they activate regions of the brain that encourage a sense of stability and safety. This helps reduce the emotional intensity that often accompanies trauma triggers, allowing the brain to engage more effectively with cognitive reframing and other therapeutic techniques.

By integrating these scientifically supported methods, R.E.S.T. not only manages trauma symptoms but also addresses the underlying neurological shifts that contribute to those symptoms. This comprehensive approach ensures that healing is not superficial but deeply rooted in the brain's ability to adapt and grow.

Time-Based Reframing: Shifting the Brain's Relationship with Time

One of the most profound ways trauma impacts the brain is through a distorted sense of time. Trauma often traps individuals in a state of feeling like the pain is eternal, that it will never end. This distorted relationship with time - where past trauma feels like it is constantly happening in the present - fuels anxiety, despair, and a belief that healing is impossible.

R.E.S.T. counters this effect through Time-Based Reframing, a process that helps survivors recognize that their current emotional state is temporary and that time, itself, is a healing force. By encouraging individuals to imagine a future where they are no longer controlled by their trauma, Time-Based Reframing helps the brain break free from the endless loop of pain. This shift not only alleviates the immediate distress but also re-engages the prefrontal cortex, giving survivors the cognitive space needed to process their trauma more effectively.

Rewiring for Resilience

Ultimately, the R.E.S.T. model is grounded in the belief that healing is possible, not just on an emotional level, but on a neurological level as well. By understanding the ways in which trauma reshapes the brain and leveraging neuroplasticity, R.E.S.T. offers a scientifically-backed, comprehensive approach to trauma recovery. It provides the tools needed to reclaim control over your thoughts and emotions, restore balance to your brain's functioning, and ultimately transform trauma into a catalyst for growth, resilience, and a deeper understanding of yourself.

Through the combined efforts of cognitive reframing, mindfulness, and time-based reframing, the brain can be rewired for healing. The R.E.S.T. model doesn't just help you survive trauma - it equips you with the neurobiological tools to thrive beyond it.

A Holistic and Personalized Recovery Path

R.E.S.T. is grounded in the belief that trauma recovery is not linear. Healing involves setbacks, breakthroughs, and long periods of seeming stagnation. The complexity of trauma means that no two recovery journeys are the same. R.E.S.T. acknowledges this and provides a customizable framework that gives you both the structure to navigate the chaos of trauma and the freedom to tailor the process to your specific needs.

At its core, the R.E.S.T. approach provides a roadmap to recovery, breaking down the overwhelming process of healing into smaller, more manageable steps. This step-by-step approach allows you to focus on one phase of healing at a time, rather than trying to tackle the enormity of your trauma all at once. As you move through the process, you'll find that each phase builds on the last, guiding you from emotional survival to deep personal transformation.

In essence, R.E.S.T. doesn't just help you cope with the trauma - it helps you grow through it. The goal is not merely to reduce symptoms, but to equip you with the tools to transform your life, fostering resilience and a deeper connection to your purpose. R.E.S.T. helps you emerge from trauma as someone who has gained wisdom, strength, and clarity, turning what once felt like a source of destruction into a foundation for rebuilding.

Moving Forward

As we've seen, trauma affects far more than just our emotions - it reshapes our very identity, alters how we perceive the world, and leaves lasting imprints on the brain's structure. The R.E.S.T. model was designed with this complexity in mind, addressing trauma from a holistic standpoint that includes emotional, cognitive, and existential healing. Understanding the science behind trauma and its effects on the brain offers hope, but the true power of healing lies in taking deliberate steps toward recovery.

The first of these steps is Release - the foundational phase of the R.E.S.T. model. Before we can begin to reframe our thinking, regain a sense of control over our lives, and find meaning in our suffering, we must first create emotional space for healing to occur. Trauma leaves us overwhelmed with intense emotions - fear, anger, guilt, shame - and these feelings often act as barriers, keeping us trapped in survival mode.

The next section will guide you through the process of releasing the emotional weight that trauma leaves behind, helping you to gradually step out of the chaos of reactivity and into a more grounded, calmer state of mind. By learning techniques such as grounding, mindfulness, and emotional processing, you will begin to shift away from the overwhelming intensity of trauma and toward a place of healing. It's here, in this first crucial step, where the journey of healing truly begins.

R.E.S.T. Practice

Applying The R.E.S.T. Method

This chapter introduces the full pathway: Release, Examine Through Time, Select What Matters, and Transform Meaning.

Release: What needs to settle before you analyze this?

____

____

____

____

Examine Through Time: How might this feel or look different with time, distance, and support?

____

____

____

____

Select What Matters: What truly deserves your energy here?

____

____

____

____

Transform Meaning: What meaning can be built without minimizing what happened?

____

____

____

____

Reflection Prompts

- Which part of R.E.S.T. feels most needed right now?

____

____

- Which part feels hardest to practice?

____

____

- What would it look like to use the method slowly rather than perfectly?

____

____

Gentle Reminder

Do not force insight before your body has enough safety to hold it. Regulation comes before interpretation. You can return to any exercise slowly, briefly, and with support.

Chapter 4

Release: Calming the Emotional Charge of Trauma

Emotionally Detaching from Trauma for Objective Analysis

Trauma doesn't just create emotional wounds; it redefines how we experience life. It alters the way we think, the way we feel, and even the way we view the world around us. For many survivors, trauma is not something that remains in the past - it continues to intrude upon the present, often without warning, pulling us back into an overwhelming emotional spiral. It can feel like an endless cycle - reliving the pain, fear, or helplessness that marked the original event. This is why trauma recovery requires more than just time; it demands intentional, guided effort to reclaim control over your emotional life.

In the R.E.S.T. framework, the first step toward breaking free from this cycle is Release. This phase focuses on emotionally detaching from the trauma so that you can begin viewing it with objectivity. The idea of emotional detachment might raise questions - why should we distance ourselves from emotions when they are part of what makes us human? The answer is simple: while emotions are essential, they can also cloud our judgment when it comes to trauma. They can distort our perception and prevent us from seeing our experiences with the clarity necessary for healing.

The emotions tied to trauma are valid and deserve recognition. However, they can also become so overwhelming that it becomes impossible to separate your identity from the traumatic experience. Learning to detach from the intense emotional charge of the trauma is vital for creating the space necessary to examine the trauma for what it is - a past event, rather than an ongoing reality.

The Emotional and Physiological Impact of Trauma

To fully understand the importance of emotional detachment, it's essential to first comprehend how trauma affects both your mind and body. Trauma isn't just a psychological event; it leaves an imprint on your nervous system, essentially reshaping how your brain functions. When you experience trauma, your brain is flooded with stress hormones like adrenaline and cortisol. These hormones are crucial for your body's fight-or-flight response, designed to help you survive immediate danger by preparing you to either confront the threat or escape it.

While this survival response is helpful in the moment, the problem arises when the brain fails to shut off this heightened state of alert after the danger has passed. For many trauma survivors, this heightened state becomes their new normal. The amygdala, the brain's emotional processing center, remains on high alert, continually scanning for potential threats. At the same time, the prefrontal cortex - the part of the brain responsible for rational thinking, planning, and decision-making - becomes less active, making it difficult to process traumatic memories in a logical or detached way.

This imbalance explains why traumatic memories often feel so vivid and overpowering. It's not just that you're remembering the event; your brain is actively reliving it as though it's happening again. This creates a constant loop where the trauma feels as though it's still unfolding in real-time. The emotional intensity tied to the trauma becomes all-consuming, leaving little room for rational thought or objective reflection.

Why Emotional Detachment is Key to Healing

This is where emotional detachment becomes a crucial tool for recovery. Emotional detachment allows you to step back from the raw intensity of these memories, creating a necessary buffer between you and the trauma. It doesn't mean denying or suppressing your emotions; rather, it enables you to engage with your trauma in a healthier, more balanced way. By developing this detachment, you create the mental and emotional space needed to observe your trauma objectively, making it possible to analyze it without being overwhelmed by it.

Imagine you are watching a movie in which the protagonist goes through a painful event. While you might empathize with the character, you're also able to observe the event with some level of emotional distance. You are not physically experiencing the pain, and this distance allows you to think critically about what is happening. Emotional detachment from trauma functions in a similar way - it creates a separation between your emotional self and the traumatic memory, allowing you to look at the trauma from a clearer perspective.

For instance, Sarah, a woman who experienced a traumatic car accident, used to feel overwhelming fear every time she thought about driving. Her body would respond as if she were back in that car, trapped, with the sound of screeching tires and the smell of burning rubber filling her senses. By learning emotional detachment, Sarah was able to observe the memory of the accident from a more objective standpoint. Instead of being immediately overwhelmed by panic, she could acknowledge, "Yes, that event was terrifying, but it is in the past. I am not in danger right now."

But emotional detachment doesn't happen automatically - it requires practice, patience, and tools. Let's explore some of the practical techniques that can help foster emotional detachment.

Grounding: A Lifeline for Emotional Overwhelm

Grounding techniques are some of the most effective tools for achieving emotional detachment. The purpose of grounding is to anchor you in the present moment, especially when your mind feels like it's being pulled back into the past by trauma. Trauma often creates a time distortion where the past feels like it's happening all over again, especially during flashbacks or moments of intense emotional overwhelm.

By grounding yourself, you remind your brain and body that you are safe right now - that the trauma is no longer happening. Grounding is about reclaiming your connection to the present, so the trauma doesn't have the power to pull you back into a cycle of fear or helplessness. It works by engaging your senses - sight, sound, touch, smell, and taste - focusing your attention outward instead of inward on the trauma.

The 5-4-3-2-1 Technique: A Grounding Exercise for Emotional Release

One of the most powerful and widely used grounding techniques is the 5-4-3-2-1 Technique. This method works by engaging all five of your senses to root you in the present moment, pulling you out of the trauma's emotional grip and into the safety of the current environment. Let's break it down in more detail:

Five things you can see: Look around the space you are in and name five things you can see. They don't have to be extraordinary - a picture on the wall, a clock ticking, the color of a table. The point is to redirect your focus from internal turmoil to external observation.

Four things you can feel: Shift your attention to physical sensations. Can you feel the chair supporting you? The fabric of your clothes against your skin? The coolness of the air? Physical sensations are a powerful way to anchor yourself, reminding your body that it is safe in the present moment.

Three things you can hear: Now, listen closely to your environment. Can you hear birds chirping outside? The hum of a refrigerator? The murmur of voices in another room? Sound is an especially grounding sense because it pulls your focus outward, away from intrusive thoughts.

Two things you can smell: Identify two distinct scents around you. It might be the familiar scent of your home, the lingering smell of food, or the fragrance of a candle. Grounding yourself through smell can be particularly effective, as scents are deeply connected to memory. However, in this context, focusing on the present smells can help sever the link between the traumatic memory and the emotional response triggered by those past events. By reconnecting with the present through your senses, you're teaching your brain that it's safe here and now.

One thing you can taste: Finally, focus on what you can taste. Perhaps it's the lingering flavor of a recent meal, the taste of coffee or tea, or even the neutral taste of your mouth. This small act of mindfulness helps anchor you in the present, bringing your awareness away from the internal chaos and toward the reality of the present.

This technique may seem simple, but it's incredibly powerful. It works because it forces the brain to shift from its state of emotional hijack back to the rational, conscious present. Each step of the 5-4-3-2-1 exercise creates a moment of space between you and the trauma. The more you practice this technique, the easier it becomes to ground yourself in the present when intrusive memories or emotional overwhelm arise.

Let's take Sarah's case a step further. In the days following her car accident, Sarah found herself constantly on edge, as though the crash could happen again at any moment. Even small triggers - like the sound of tires screeching on the road - would send her into a state of panic. Through practicing the 5-4-3-2-1 technique, Sarah learned how to ground herself during those moments of fear. Each time she heard the screech of tires and felt her heart race, she would focus on her immediate surroundings. She might notice the color of the sky, feel the seat under her, or listen to the sound of her own breathing. Over time, this practice helped Sarah reduce the intensity of her triggers and regain a sense of control over her emotions.

Why Grounding is More Than a Temporary Fix

Grounding exercises like the 5-4-3-2-1 technique offer immediate relief, but their benefits extend far beyond the moment. With regular practice, grounding rewires your brain's response to trauma-related triggers. Instead of defaulting to panic, fear, or emotional overload, your brain gradually learns to engage the prefrontal cortex - the area responsible for rational thinking - more effectively. This makes it easier to stay calm, even when faced with reminders of the trauma.

Moreover, grounding exercises help develop neural pathways that promote emotional regulation. The more you practice grounding, the more efficient your body becomes at activating its calming mechanisms. Over time, grounding transforms from a conscious effort into an automatic response, creating long-lasting resilience against trauma triggers.

Deep Breathing: Resetting Your Emotional Response

While grounding helps you focus on the present, deep breathing is a tool that works to reset your physiological response to trauma. Trauma can trigger a physical reaction in the body, causing the fight-or-flight response to kick in. When this happens, your breathing often becomes shallow and rapid, signaling to your brain that you're still in danger. Deep breathing, however, sends the opposite message: "I am safe."

Deep, slow breathing activates the parasympathetic nervous system, which is responsible for calming the body. It stimulates the vagus nerve, which runs from the brainstem through the neck and into the abdomen. This nerve is a key player in regulating the body's stress response, and by stimulating it through deep breathing, you can lower your heart rate, reduce muscle tension, and calm your mind.

Let's break down a simple but highly effective deep breathing exercise that you can use alongside grounding:

The 4-7-8 Breathing Technique

This technique is designed to help regulate your breath and slow down your body's stress response. It works by extending your exhalation, which activates the body's relaxation response. Here's how it works:

Inhale for a count of 4: Breathe in deeply through your nose for a count of four. Focus on filling your lungs completely, expanding your diaphragm.

Hold for a count of 7: After the inhale, hold your breath for a count of seven. This holding phase helps your body fully absorb the oxygen and engage the vagus nerve.

Exhale for a count of 8: Slowly exhale through your mouth for a count of eight. Make sure to empty your lungs completely as you do this.

Repeat: Complete the cycle at least three times, or until you begin to feel more relaxed.

The extended exhalation is key here - it signals to your body that it's time to relax and de-escalates the fight-or-flight response. You can use this technique anytime you feel emotionally overwhelmed or notice the early signs of a trauma response, like a racing heart, shallow breathing, or muscle tension.

Long-Term Benefits of Deep Breathing

Beyond the immediate calming effect, regular practice of deep breathing offers long-term benefits. By consistently engaging the parasympathetic nervous system, deep breathing trains your body to respond to stress more efficiently. Over time, this can reduce the frequency and intensity of trauma-related reactions, giving you greater control over how you respond to emotional triggers.

For example, consider Jason, a war veteran who struggled with panic attacks triggered by loud noises. Every time he heard a car backfire or fireworks in the distance, his body would immediately tense up, and his breathing would become shallow, leading to a full-blown panic attack. After working with a therapist to incorporate deep breathing techniques like the 4-7-8 method, Jason was able to retrain his body to respond differently. Now, when he hears a loud noise, he automatically takes a deep breath and holds it before exhaling slowly. Over time, this simple practice has helped reduce his panic attacks and allowed him to feel more grounded in everyday life.

Building a Foundation for Objective Analysis

Once you've practiced grounding and deep breathing regularly, and have begun to emotionally detach from your trauma, you're ready for the next phase: Objective Analysis. Emotional detachment creates the necessary space to view your trauma with greater objectivity. This distance is what allows you to start analyzing the trauma without being consumed by it. It's this objectivity that lays the foundation for reframing your trauma - not as an all-consuming event, but as a stepping stone for growth and healing.

Think of trauma as a thick fog. In the middle of it, everything is blurred, chaotic, and overwhelming. Your sense of reality becomes distorted because you're stuck in the middle of intense emotional responses. By practicing grounding techniques and deep breathing, you lift that fog - at least momentarily. You start to see your trauma from a distance, and for the first time, you can begin to engage with it without being emotionally overwhelmed.

This objective space is crucial for moving forward. Without it, trauma continues to have power over you, and you remain stuck in reactive patterns - constantly reliving the emotional intensity of the experience. Objective analysis shifts you out of that reactive state and into one of reflection and, eventually, understanding.

But why is objectivity so important when it comes to trauma recovery? Trauma, by nature, distorts perception. It creates emotional flashpoints, making it difficult to separate what happened from how you feel about what happened. These emotions - fear, anger, sadness, guilt - are often overwhelming, blurring the line between past and present. When you're caught in this emotional vortex, it can feel as though the trauma is ongoing, as though you are forever tethered to the moment it occurred. This is where Objective Analysis becomes transformative.

Detachment Doesn't Mean Indifference

It's important to clarify what emotional detachment does and doesn't mean. Detachment, in this context, isn't about becoming indifferent to your trauma or pretending that it didn't happen. Emotional detachment is a way of creating space between you and the overwhelming emotions tied to the trauma so that you can approach it with greater clarity. It allows you to step back, not to distance yourself from the importance of the event, but to give yourself the mental clarity to process it.

This process isn't about devaluing your emotions or detaching from them permanently. Instead, it's about learning to observe your feelings without being controlled by them. Trauma-related emotions are valid, but when they run unchecked, they can dominate your experience of the world. Emotional detachment allows you to create a buffer between the intensity of your feelings and your capacity for objective thought, so you can begin to see the trauma in a new light.

The emotional distance you achieve through detachment is the space in which healing happens. It's where you can begin to dissect the trauma, understand its components, and, eventually, transform it.

The First Steps of Objective Analysis: Changing the Narrative

Now that you've learned to ground yourself in the present and regulate your emotional responses through deep breathing, the next step is learning how to change the narrative of your trauma. This is the essence of objective analysis - moving from viewing the trauma as a dominating force to seeing it as one part of your life's story.

In the fog of trauma, it's easy to think of yourself solely in terms of what you've suffered. But in truth, trauma is not the whole story of who you are; it's one chapter. Objective analysis helps you pull back and see this bigger picture. While trauma can feel like it defines everything, you are more than your worst moments. This is the first shift in perspective that comes with objective analysis.

Imagine your life as a book. The trauma is a chapter - an important one, certainly, but not the entire story. With objective analysis, you begin to see the other chapters again: your strengths, your resilience, your relationships, your passions, your goals. This broader perspective helps reduce the emotional weight of the trauma because you begin to see that it doesn't define you.

Creating Emotional Distance Through Visualization

One technique that can help build emotional distance and lay the groundwork for objective analysis is visualization. This involves consciously stepping into the role of an observer, rather than a participant, in your trauma narrative.

Exercise: Visualizing the Trauma From a Distance

Close your eyes and imagine your trauma as a movie playing on a screen in front of you. You are seated in a theater, watching the events unfold, but you are not inside the movie. You are an observer, safe and detached from the emotional intensity of what's happening on the screen.

As you watch the events play out, focus on maintaining your role as an observer. If you start to feel pulled into the emotions of the memory, take a deep breath and remind yourself that you are safe - you're in the present, watching the past from a distance.

After the "movie" ends, take a moment to reflect on the experience from your observer's perspective. How did it feel to view the trauma from this distance? Did anything stand out to you that you hadn't noticed before?

Visualization is a powerful tool for creating emotional distance because it trains your brain to engage with the trauma in a controlled, mindful way. Instead of being swept up by the emotions, you're able to watch the event unfold, creating the space needed for objective reflection.

Anchoring Objectivity in the Present

One of the challenges of trauma recovery is that the emotional intensity of the past often bleeds into the present. You might find yourself reacting to everyday situations as though the trauma is still happening, leading to heightened anxiety, hypervigilance, or emotional overwhelm. Objective analysis requires anchoring yourself in the present so that you can begin to differentiate between the past and the now.

Grounding techniques are invaluable for anchoring yourself in the present, but another essential component is temporal awareness - the ability to recognize that the trauma is in the past and that you are not in immediate danger. By reminding yourself that you are in control of your present reality, you begin to diminish the power of trauma memories to intrude on your current emotional state.

Building Emotional Resilience for Objective Analysis

To successfully engage in objective analysis, you need to cultivate emotional resilience - the ability to confront difficult memories or emotions without being overwhelmed by them. Emotional resilience doesn't mean you never feel pain or discomfort, but rather that you have the tools to manage those feelings when they arise.

Emotional resilience can be developed through:

Mindfulness: Staying connected to the present moment helps prevent the emotional hijacking that trauma can cause. Regular mindfulness practices, like meditation or mindful walking, can strengthen your ability to stay grounded, even when confronted with painful memories.

Self-Compassion: One of the most important components of emotional resilience is self-compassion - the ability to treat yourself with kindness and understanding when you're struggling. Trauma often brings with it harsh self-judgment, but learning to replace this judgment with compassion is a key step in building resilience.

Support Systems: Emotional resilience is often strengthened by supportive relationships. Whether it's a trusted friend, family member, or therapist, having someone to talk to can make a big difference in your ability to process trauma. These relationships provide a safe space for you to express emotions and reflect on your progress without fear of judgment.

The Power of Objective Analysis in Reframing Trauma

As you continue practicing emotional detachment and building resilience, objective analysis becomes more effective. Once you're able to see your trauma from a distance, you can begin to question the negative beliefs or thought patterns it has created. This is the foundation of reframing - a process that will allow you to transform your trauma into a source of strength and empowerment, rather than a source of suffering.

Real-World Example: Sarah's Journey Through R.E.S.T.

To illustrate how the Release phase can transform your relationship with trauma, let's delve deeper into Sarah's story. After a traumatic car accident, Sarah's life was overwhelmed by the aftershocks of fear and anxiety. What was once a simple drive to work became a harrowing ordeal, filled with panic attacks and flashbacks. The mere thought of getting behind the wheel or passing the intersection where the accident occurred sent her into a spiral of dread. The trauma didn't just affect her driving - it consumed her daily life. Sounds as common as screeching tires or even the hum of traffic lights would trigger flashbacks, pulling her back into that moment of terror.

The All-Consuming Nature of Trauma

For Sarah, her trauma was not just a memory. It was a persistent, involuntary re-living of the accident, a reminder of her helplessness during that moment. Each time she was exposed to a reminder - whether it was the sound of tires, the feel of the steering wheel, or simply driving near the site of the crash - her body would react as if the accident were happening all over again. Her heart would race, her breathing would become shallow, and she would feel like she was losing control of herself. These physical responses made it impossible for her to distinguish between the past and the present, and as a result, her life became increasingly restricted.

She avoided driving whenever possible, relying on others for rides and taking public transport even when it was inconvenient. But the world around her didn't stop presenting triggers - passing cars, honking horns, and sudden noises constantly reminded her of that day. Over time, her world shrank, and she began to feel imprisoned by her fear. The trauma had not only taken over her mind but also controlled her actions, dictating how she lived her life. Sarah knew she had to break free from this cycle, but she didn't know how.

Grounding Techniques

When Sarah began working on her trauma recovery, the first thing she learned was the 5-4-3-2-1 grounding technique, a powerful tool that allowed her to anchor herself in the present moment. She learned that trauma makes the past feel as if it's happening in the present, and her brain had become conditioned to react to perceived threats even when none existed. The grounding exercise helped her reconnect to her immediate surroundings and pull herself out of the emotional loop.

The next time she was driving and felt the familiar panic rise in her chest, Sarah consciously used the technique. As her fear began to spike, she immediately shifted her focus away from the trigger and onto her surroundings:

5 Things She Could See: She scanned her environment and focused on the trees lining the road, the clouds in the sky, the rearview mirror, the stop sign ahead, and the cars around her.

4 Things She Could Feel: She brought her awareness to the feel of the steering wheel in her hands, the seatbelt across her chest, the pressure of her foot on the brake, and the texture of her jacket.

3 Things She Could Hear: She listened for the hum of the car engine, the sound of birds outside, and the low murmur of the radio.

2 Things She Could Smell: She noticed the scent of her coffee in the cup holder and the fresh air coming through the window.

1 Thing She Could Taste: She became aware of the minty aftertaste of her gum.

The exercise allowed Sarah to pull herself back from the brink of panic. Instead of spiraling into memories of the accident, she was able to stay grounded in the here and now. The world around her was no longer a chaotic threat but a place where she was in control.

Learning Emotional Detachment

As Sarah continued practicing these grounding techniques, she started noticing a subtle shift. While she still felt anxiety when driving, she was no longer completely overwhelmed by it. She was creating space between herself and the emotional intensity of her trauma. This space allowed her to start seeing her reactions more objectively. Instead of thinking, "I'm panicking because I'm about to have another accident," she could begin to say, "I'm safe right now, and this fear is just my mind reacting to the past." This change in thinking was the first step toward emotional detachment.

Over time, Sarah started using deep breathing exercises in tandem with grounding. Whenever she felt the anxiety rise, she would take slow, deep breaths, counting to four as she inhaled, holding for four seconds, and then exhaling for another count of four. This calmed her racing heart and helped quiet her mind. Slowly but surely, Sarah was learning how to take control of her body's responses to triggers. She no longer felt like a helpless passenger being driven by her trauma. Instead, she was taking back the wheel, both literally and figuratively.

Building Emotional Distance

With consistent practice, Sarah's emotional detachment became more robust. Her flashbacks, though still present, began to lose their emotional grip. When she passed the intersection where the accident had occurred, she still felt a pang of anxiety, but it was no longer paralyzing. She could observe the anxiety without being consumed by it. She could now say to herself, "This is the place where the accident happened, but I'm not in danger anymore."

Sarah's progress wasn't linear. Some days, she still felt overwhelmed by the memories, and there were moments when panic would resurface unexpectedly. But the more she practiced grounding and emotional detachment, the more resilient she became. Even when she had setbacks, she knew she had tools she could rely on to bring herself back to the present.

Reframing the Trauma Through Objective Analysis

Once Sarah had developed enough emotional distance from her trauma, she was able to begin the next phase: Objective Analysis. This didn't happen overnight. But over time, Sarah's ability to view the trauma with a clearer, more objective lens improved, allowing her to step back and examine the accident in a new way. The accident had been a chaotic, terrifying event, and for a long time, Sarah viewed it solely as a source of pain and fear. But now, she could ask different kinds of questions:

What did I do to keep myself safe during the accident? Sarah remembered how she had instinctively swerved to avoid a more serious collision. In the midst of chaos, her instincts had kicked in, helping to protect her.

How did I manage to recover physically after the accident? Though the recovery process was slow and painful, Sarah realized she had demonstrated resilience. She followed through with physical therapy, endured setbacks, and regained her mobility.

What can I learn from this experience to help me move forward? Rather than allowing the accident to define her, Sarah began to see it as a point of growth. She had survived. She had learned that even in the most terrifying moments, she could trust herself to take action and protect her well-being.

By engaging with these questions, Sarah reframed her narrative. No longer was she simply the victim of a terrible event - she was a survivor who had navigated a life-threatening situation and come out stronger. This shift in perspective allowed Sarah to feel a new sense of empowerment. The accident was no longer the central, all-consuming event of her life. Instead, it became a chapter in a much larger story - one that included resilience, strength, and personal growth.

Moving Toward Reclaiming Control

Sarah's journey through the Release phase of the R.E.S.T. framework illustrates how emotionally detaching from trauma and engaging in objective analysis can create the space needed for reframing. By stepping back from the emotional intensity of the trauma, she was able to shift her focus from what happened to her to how she responded to it. This shift is crucial for trauma survivors because it transforms the narrative from one of victimhood to one of agency and empowerment.

Through grounding and deep breathing, Sarah learned to regulate her emotions in the face of triggers. Through emotional detachment, she created the space necessary to observe her trauma without being overwhelmed by it. And through objective analysis, she was able to begin rewriting her story - one where she wasn't defined by her trauma but by her resilience.

In the next phase of R.E.S.T., Sarah will focus on Time-Based Reframing, learning to place her trauma in the broader context of time. This will help her understand that while the trauma was a significant event, it is not the defining feature of her life. Temporal reframing will allow her to continue this process of growth, further disentangling herself from the emotional grip of the past while building a future grounded in strength and healing.

R.E.S.T. Practice

Applying Release: Calming the Emotional Charge of Trauma

This chapter helps you steady the body and create enough emotional distance to think clearly without suppressing or denying what you feel.

Release: What needs to settle before you analyze this?

____

____

____

____

Examine Through Time: How might this feel or look different with time, distance, and support?

____

____

____

____

Select What Matters: What truly deserves your energy here?

____

____

____

____

Transform Meaning: What meaning can be built without minimizing what happened?

____

____

____

____

Reflection Prompts

- What helps my body feel even five percent safer?

____

____

- What do I usually do when I become emotionally flooded?

____

____

- What would it mean to delay interpretation until I am more regulated?

____

____

Gentle Reminder

Do not force insight before your body has enough safety to hold it. Regulation comes before interpretation. You can return to any exercise slowly, briefly, and with support.

Daily Micro-Practice

Release

Use this page as a brief daily practice. The point is repetition, not perfection. One honest sentence is enough.

Today I noticed:

____

____

____

____

The trauma-shaped story that appeared was:

____

____

____

____

The R.E.S.T. response I want to practice is:

____

____

____

____

One gentle action I can take next is:

____

____

____

____

Chapter 5

Examine Through Time: Seeing Pain Beyond the Present Moment

The Concept of Time-Based Reframing

Imagine a painting - large and vivid, filled with intricate details. If you stand too close, you only see a small section of the artwork. Your focus is limited to one particular corner, one stroke of the brush. You miss the fullness of the painting's beauty, the way the colors blend, the way the individual parts come together to form a cohesive whole. In the same way, when we are too close to our pain, we only see that one part of our emotional experience. The sadness, the fear, or the anxiety becomes the entire picture, and we forget that this moment is just one part of a much larger canvas.

Time-Based Reframing is the process of stepping back from that small section and widening our view. It's about understanding that while this moment of pain is real and significant, it is not the entirety of our story. Time provides the emotional distance we need to gain perspective, to see that what feels overwhelming today will not feel as heavy tomorrow, next week, or a year from now.

The key question behind Time-Based Reframing is, "How will I feel about this in the future?" This is not a question meant to diminish your current pain or rush you toward healing. Instead, it is a gentle reminder that your relationship with this moment will evolve. The feelings that seem so overpowering right now are not fixed; they are fluid, and time will naturally reshape them.

The Psychology Behind Time-Based Reframing: How Time Heals

To understand why Time-Based Reframing works, we need to dive deeper into the way the human brain processes emotions over time. In the immediate aftermath of a traumatic or painful event, the brain is flooded with intense emotions. It triggers a response in the amygdala, the part of the brain responsible for processing fear and threats. This response is crucial for survival in moments of real danger, but it can also magnify emotional experiences, making them feel far more overwhelming than they actually are.

When you're experiencing intense emotions - whether it's grief, anger, anxiety, or despair - it's easy for the mind to become trapped in what cognitive psychologists call "emotional reasoning." This is when we start to believe that the way we feel in the moment is a reflection of reality, leading us to think, "I feel overwhelmed, so my life must be overwhelming," or, "I feel hopeless, so my situation must be hopeless." Emotional reasoning distorts our perspective and makes it difficult to see beyond the present pain.

However, the brain has an incredible capacity for neuroplasticity - the ability to change and adapt over time. As time passes, the intensity of the emotional response begins to decrease. The brain starts to process and integrate the painful experience into the larger narrative of our lives, often giving it new meaning and context. This is why, when we look back on past experiences, we often find that the emotions we felt so intensely in the moment have softened or shifted. We may even find value or growth in those experiences that we couldn't see at the time.

Time-Based Reframing harnesses this natural process by encouraging you to project yourself into the future, where time has had a chance to do its work. By visualizing your future self - a self that has healed, learned, and gained perspective - you can begin to see that the emotional storm you're in right now is not permanent. Time is a powerful healer, and by engaging with this process consciously, you can create a sense of hope and resilience in the present.

The Goal of Time-Based Reframing: Hope, Patience, and Emotional Distance

The primary goal of Time-Based Reframing is to foster hope and patience. It's about reminding yourself that no matter how overwhelming your emotions may feel right now, they are temporary. The intensity of your pain, anxiety, or grief will not last forever. By imagining your future self - someone who has had time to heal and process - you give yourself permission to trust in the natural process of emotional recovery.

Time-Based Reframing also helps create emotional distance. When we are caught up in the immediacy of our emotions, it's hard to see beyond the present moment. We become consumed by the fear that our pain will never end. But by projecting yourself into the future, you can step outside of that narrow view and recognize that this too shall pass.

Patience is a key aspect of Time-Based Reframing. It teaches us that healing takes time and that there is no need to rush through the pain. By trusting in the passage of time, we learn to sit with our emotions without being overwhelmed by them, knowing that things will change. The very act of imagining a future where the pain has softened helps to reduce its intensity in the present.

How to Practice Time-Based Reframing: A Step-by-Step Guide

Here's a guide to help you practice Time-Based Reframing in your own life. This technique can be applied in moments of acute emotional distress, but it can also be used as an ongoing tool to reshape your relationship with difficult experiences over time.

Step 1: Acknowledge the Present Pain

The first step in Time-Based Reframing is to acknowledge the intensity of what you are feeling. Name the emotion - whether it's grief, fear, anger, or sadness - and recognize that it is a natural response to the situation you're facing. Don't rush to push the emotion away or pretend it isn't there. Instead, give yourself permission to feel it fully, knowing that this is an important part of the healing process.

For example, if you're dealing with a breakup, you might say to yourself, "This hurts. I feel heartbroken, and that's okay." Acknowledging the pain doesn't mean you're surrendering to it; it simply means that you're giving yourself the space to experience it without judgment.

Step 2: Visualize Your Future Self

Once you've acknowledged your present emotions, the next step is to project yourself into the future. Imagine yourself six months, a year, or even five years from now. Visualize what your life might look like at that point. Who are you? What have you learned? How have you healed from this experience?

Try to paint a vivid picture of your future self - someone who has gained emotional distance from the current pain, someone who has grown stronger because of the experience. This future version of you isn't free from pain, but they have learned to live with it in a way that no longer defines them.

For example, if you're struggling with the loss of a job, imagine your future self in a new role, one that better aligns with your values and goals. Imagine the growth you've experienced since losing your previous job - the resilience you've built, the skills you've acquired, the new opportunities that have come your way.

Step 3: Reflect on the Passage of Time

Take a moment to reflect on how time naturally changes emotions. Think about previous experiences in your life that once felt overwhelming - moments of loss, failure, or disappointment. How do you feel about those moments now, with the benefit of hindsight?

Perhaps what once seemed devastating no longer holds the same emotional charge. Perhaps you've even found meaning or growth in those experiences. Use this reflection to remind yourself that your relationship with your current pain will also change over time. The emotions you're feeling today will not feel the same tomorrow.

Step 4: Reframe the Present

Now that you've visualized your future self and reflected on how time changes emotions, bring that awareness back to the present. Reframe the current moment by reminding yourself that while the pain is real, it is not permanent.

You might say to yourself, "This is difficult right now, but I know that with time, I will heal. I will look back on this moment with new understanding. I have survived difficult moments before, and I will survive this too."

By reframing the present through the lens of time, you can create a sense of hope and emotional resilience. The pain no longer feels as overwhelming because you know that it is just one part of your journey, not the whole of it.

Step 5: Trust in the Process of Healing

Finally, the most important step in Time-Based Reframing is to trust the process of time. Healing takes time, and there's no rushing it. By practicing patience and giving yourself permission to move through the emotions at your own pace, you allow the natural process of recovery to unfold.

Remember, time is a force that constantly shapes and reshapes our lives. By trusting in its power, you can approach even the most difficult moments with a sense of hope and resilience.

Example: Applying Time-Based Reframing to Daily Life

Let's explore how Time-Based Reframing can be a powerful tool to navigate overwhelming emotions during moments of crisis by walking through the experience of someone facing profound personal hardship.

Imagine Sarah, a mother of two, who has recently gone through a heartbreaking divorce after nearly a decade of marriage. In the days and weeks following the separation, Sarah finds herself drowning in a sea of emotions - guilt, sadness, fear, and an overwhelming sense of failure. She feels as though the ground has been ripped out from beneath her, and she's left floating aimlessly, unsure of how to rebuild her life.

Every night, after putting her children to bed, she lies awake, staring at the ceiling, feeling the weight of the world pressing down on her. Sleepless nights have become routine. Her mind is consumed by relentless thoughts: "What if I've ruined everything? What if my children resent me for this? What if I'm never happy again?" The "what ifs" feel endless, and her emotional pain grows heavier with each passing day. At times, the grief and self-doubt become so intense that it feels as though her life will never get better.

"Will I ever feel normal again?" she wonders, staring at her reflection in the bathroom mirror, a version of herself she barely recognizes. She feels stuck, trapped in a painful cycle, unable to see beyond the sorrow that seems to define her every waking moment.

In this fragile emotional state, Sarah could easily remain overwhelmed by her feelings, but she decides to turn to a Time-Based

Reframing exercise as a tool to help her break free from the intensity of the moment. Rather than running away from her emotions or trying to force herself to "move on" prematurely, Time-Based Reframing invites Sarah to face her pain, sit with it, and begin to shift her perspective.

Step 1: Acknowledging the Present Pain

Sarah starts by acknowledging the depth of her pain. She knows she cannot skip over it or suppress it, as that will only make it stronger. Instead, she chooses to confront it, to hold her pain with compassion rather than judgment. She sits in a quiet corner of her living room, clutching a warm cup of tea, and says to herself: "This hurts so much. I feel devastated. I'm afraid for my children, and I feel like I've failed everyone, including myself."

In this moment, Sarah gives herself the space to fully feel her emotions without rushing through them or labeling them as "bad." There is no judgment here, only acceptance. She acknowledges that her heartache is real and profound - this was the end of a life she had once envisioned, a marriage she had hoped would last forever. She lets the sadness wash over her, understanding that allowing herself to feel the pain is part of the healing process.

This acknowledgment, though difficult, is a crucial step in Time-Based Reframing. It sets the foundation of self-compassion. Rather than shaming herself for feeling vulnerable, Sarah recognizes that what she is experiencing is a natural human response to loss.

Step 2: Visualizing the Future Self

Once Sarah has given herself permission to grieve, she moves to the next step in Time-Based Reframing: visualizing her future self. She closes her eyes and imagines what her life might look like a year from now. At first, it feels difficult to envision any kind of joy in the future, but she persists, knowing that time will help ease her pain.

In her mind's eye, she sees herself in a bright kitchen, cooking dinner with her children. Laughter fills the room, the sound of her kids happily playing nearby, their smiles lighting up her heart. She sees herself stronger, more resilient, and at peace with the decision to leave her marriage. She is no longer defined by her divorce, but by how she has grown from the experience. Sarah imagines herself rebuilding her life - not just surviving, but thriving.

In this vision, Sarah has reclaimed her sense of self. She is pursuing a career that brings her fulfillment, and she has created a home filled with warmth and stability. There are moments of happiness with her children, where they are adjusting well to the changes. Sarah sees them flourishing - doing well in school, enjoying time with friends, and most importantly, feeling safe and loved.

"It's not perfect," she reminds herself, "but it's a life I've built with intention, one where my children and I are okay." She doesn't expect her future to be free from challenges, but she sees herself as someone who has learned to adapt, who can navigate life's uncertainties with grace.

This future version of herself is not a distant fantasy - it's a realistic vision grounded in the truth that time has the power to heal and transform. Sarah knows she won't wake up tomorrow and feel completely better, but she trusts that a year from now, the pain will not be as sharp. She trusts that she will have found her footing again.

Step 3: Reflecting on Past Growth

With this future vision in mind, Sarah reflects on her past, recalling times when she felt similarly lost and overwhelmed. She remembers when she was a new mother, sleepless nights spent with a crying baby in her arms, wondering if she'd ever find her way. She remembers the difficult transitions in her career, the setbacks that made her doubt her abilities, and even the moments when financial strain seemed like an insurmountable burden.

Back then, she thought the challenges were impossible to overcome. "How am I ever going to get through this?" she had asked herself, just as she's asking now. But somehow, she had made it through those difficult periods. With the passage of time, she grew stronger, gained new skills, and learned how to adapt. Her pain from those moments didn't disappear, but it changed shape - it became a part of her story, one that added to her resilience rather than detracted from it.

"I've survived hard things before," she reminds herself, "and I'll survive this too." Just as time helped her heal in the past, she believes that it will help her heal now.

Step 4: Reframing the Present

Finally, Sarah brings the wisdom from her future vision and her past reflections back into the present. She sits quietly for a moment, taking a deep breath and exhaling slowly. The pain she feels is still real, but it no longer consumes her. By viewing her current emotions through the lens of time, she starts to feel lighter, less burdened by the immediacy of the pain.

"I will heal," she tells herself. "This pain won't last forever. A year from now, I will look back on this moment and see how far I've come."

By reframing her emotions in this way, Sarah creates emotional distance from the intensity of the present moment. The pain is still there, but it no longer feels like an immovable weight. She sees it as part of a larger process - one that will eventually lead to healing, growth, and a deeper understanding of herself.

Sarah understands now that while she cannot control everything that happens in her life, she can control how she chooses to view her pain. She may not have the answers today, but she trusts that time will bring clarity, healing, and new opportunities for joy. With this shift in perspective, she takes her first step toward reclaiming her life.

The Long-Term Benefits of Time-Based Reframing

The true beauty of Time-Based Reframing is not just in its immediate ability to create emotional distance and offer relief during moments of acute pain, but in its profound long-term impact. As you continue to practice this technique, you begin to internalize a fundamental truth: no emotional state is permanent. This realization alone can be life-changing. It gives you the freedom to experience your emotions fully without becoming trapped by them.

Through repeated engagement with Time-Based Reframing, you cultivate a mindset grounded in resilience, patience, and hope. You develop the capacity to step back from difficult emotions and observe them with a sense of perspective, knowing that time has the power to transform even the most overwhelming feelings. This isn't about dismissing or minimizing pain - quite the opposite. Time-Based Reframing allows you to honor your emotions while also recognizing that they are part of a larger, ever-evolving journey. And within that journey, time is your ally.

Let's explore how the long-term practice of Time-Based Reframing can transform the way you navigate emotional challenges and shape your approach to life's inevitable hardships.

1. Emotional Resilience: Strengthening Your Inner Foundation

One of the most significant long-term benefits of Time-Based Reframing is the development of emotional resilience. Life is filled with moments of uncertainty, loss, and difficulty, and it's easy to feel overwhelmed by the intensity of these experiences. However, by practicing Time-Based Reframing, you learn to create a buffer between yourself and the emotional storms that arise. Over time, this practice builds an inner foundation of strength - one that allows you to face life's challenges without being consumed by them.

As you continue to use Time-Based Reframing, you realize that your emotions, no matter how intense, are not permanent. You begin to trust that while your feelings in the moment are valid and real, they will eventually soften with the passage of time. This knowledge allows you to navigate emotional pain with greater ease, knowing that healing is already in motion. Instead of being stuck in the belief that your pain will last forever, you approach hardship with the understanding that you have survived before and you will survive again. This mindset fosters a sense of confidence and resilience, empowering you to confront life's difficulties with an open heart and mind.

Over time, Time-Based Reframing shifts your relationship with adversity. Instead of reacting with fear or despair, you develop the ability to pause, reflect, and reframe, creating a more balanced emotional response. This resilience doesn't mean that you will never feel pain again - pain is a natural part of life - but it does mean that you will have the tools to navigate it with a sense of control and hope.

Resilience is not about avoiding hardship but about learning to bend without breaking.

2. Cultivating Hope: Trusting in the Possibility of Change

At the heart of Time-Based Reframing is the cultivation of hope. By regularly visualizing your future self - someone who has healed, grown, and gained perspective - you strengthen your belief in the possibility of change. Hope becomes an integral part of your emotional landscape, guiding you through moments of darkness by reminding you that light always returns.

Hope is not a naive expectation that life will be free from challenges, nor is it a denial of the pain you may be experiencing. Instead, it is a deeply rooted belief that things will get better with time, that your suffering will eventually evolve into something more manageable, and that with patience and perseverance, you can emerge from hardship stronger and wiser.

When you engage in Time-Based Reframing, you actively remind yourself that life is fluid, not static. Just as your emotions have changed in the past, they will continue to shift in the future. This sense of hope helps you endure the present moment, knowing that it is temporary and that your future holds new possibilities for healing, joy, and personal growth.

In the long term, this hopeful mindset allows you to approach life with a greater sense of optimism and curiosity. You no longer fear the uncertainty of the future because you trust that, no matter what challenges come your way, you have the inner strength to navigate them. Hope becomes a driving force, empowering you to take action in your life, seek out opportunities for growth, and continue moving forward, even when the path feels difficult.

3. Fostering Self-Compassion: Learning to Be Gentle with Yourself

Another transformative aspect of Time-Based Reframing is the development of self-compassion. So often, we are harsh with ourselves in moments of pain, believing that we should "move on" quickly or "get over" difficult emotions. But Time-Based Reframing teaches you that healing is not something that can be rushed - it is a process that unfolds in its own time.

As you practice Time-Based Reframing, you learn to treat yourself with the same kindness and patience that you would offer a dear friend. You begin to understand that it is okay to feel pain, to take time to heal, and to experience setbacks along the way. This self-compassion becomes a powerful antidote to self-criticism and guilt, allowing you to move through life with a sense of gentleness toward yourself.

Over time, Time-Based Reframing helps you recognize that emotional recovery is not linear. There will be days when the pain feels distant and days when it feels fresh again. And that's okay. The long-term benefit of this practice is that it allows you to navigate these ups and downs without judgment, trusting that each day brings you closer to healing, even if it doesn't always feel that way in the moment.

With self-compassion as a foundation, you begin to build a deeper connection with yourself. You start to honor your emotional needs, giving yourself permission to rest when you need to, cry when you need to, and reach out for support when you need it. This ongoing practice of self-compassion strengthens your emotional well-being, allowing you to face life's challenges with a greater sense of inner peace and resilience.

4. Gaining a New Perspective on Pain: Transforming Suffering into Growth

Perhaps one of the most profound long-term benefits of Time-Based Reframing is the way it transforms your perspective on pain. Over time, you begin to understand that pain, while difficult, is not something to be feared or avoided. Instead, you start to see pain as an integral part of the human experience, one that has the potential to shape you in meaningful ways.

Time-Based Reframing helps you recognize that pain does not define you, but it can become a source of growth, insight, and transformation. When you reframe your emotional experiences through the lens of time, you begin to see your hardships as stepping stones on the path to personal development. You start to ask yourself, "What can

I learn from this experience? How will this pain shape me into a stronger, wiser version of myself?"

Over time, this shift in perspective allows you to approach future challenges with a sense of curiosity and openness. You no longer fear pain because you trust that it will lead to growth. You understand that suffering, while difficult, often brings with it profound lessons about resilience, empathy, and the importance of connection.

By embracing this new perspective, you cultivate a sense of emotional flexibility - the ability to move through life's ups and downs with grace, knowing that every experience, no matter how painful, has the potential to contribute to your personal evolution. Time-Based Reframing becomes a tool for self-discovery, helping you transform suffering into something that enriches your life rather than diminishes it.

Embracing the Transformative Power of Time

The long-term benefits of Time-Based Reframing go far beyond temporary relief. This practice fundamentally shifts the way you relate to your emotions, your pain, and your journey through life. By engaging regularly with Time-Based Reframing, you create a mindset of resilience, hope, and self-compassion that becomes woven into the fabric of your emotional life. You learn to trust in the healing power of time, understanding that no matter how intense your current emotions may feel, they are part of an evolving process - one that will lead to growth, transformation, and renewed strength.

Time-Based Reframing invites you to take an active role in your healing, to engage with your future self, and to view your current pain through a broader lens. Over time, this practice will not only help you navigate the challenges of the present but will also reshape your relationship with hardship, enabling you to approach life with a sense of hope, courage, and emotional resilience.

By embracing the transformative power of time, you can move through life's inevitable difficulties with the knowledge that change is always possible, that healing is already underway, and that your future holds the potential for new beginnings, growth, and deeper meaning.

Time as a Catalyst for Healing

One of the most enduring truths about the human experience is that time is a natural healer. It doesn't erase what has happened, nor does it undo the trauma or stress that you've endured, but it has the undeniable power to soften the edges of pain, to help us see our suffering from a wider lens, and to reshape the way we relate to it. Time-Based Reframing harnesses this power of time, offering a framework through which we can transform our relationship with pain, stress, and trauma. It teaches us that no matter how overwhelming the present moment feels, time itself will bring new perspectives, insights, and healing.

When you engage in Time-Based Reframing, you step outside the immediate emotional intensity of the present and look toward a future where healing has already begun to take place. It encourages you to think of yourself as someone who is still in motion - still becoming, still growing, still capable of change. The pain you feel today is real, but time teaches us that it is not eternal. Over time, the sharpness of grief dulls, the weight of stress lightens, and what once seemed impossible to bear becomes something you can carry with more ease.

The beauty of Time-Based Reframing lies in its ability to create emotional distance between you and the hardship you're experiencing. By imagining your future self - someone who has gained wisdom and strength through the experience - you are reminded that the emotional intensity you feel now will shift. The passage of time allows your emotions to breathe, to evolve, and to transform into something more manageable, less consuming.

This process requires two essential qualities: patience and trust. Patience is the understanding that healing is not immediate - it is gradual, unfolding in its own time. There will be setbacks and days where the pain resurfaces, but the trajectory is one of healing and growth. Trust is the belief that, as time passes, you will gain clarity and insight. You trust that your future self will have the benefit of distance and perspective, which will allow you to understand this moment in a different light.

As time moves forward, so do you. You begin to recognize that your pain, while significant, is just one chapter in the larger narrative of your life. It does not define the whole of who you are. In the space that time creates, you find room for new experiences, for joy, for meaning, and for a future that is not weighed down by the past. Time-Based Reframing is not about dismissing your pain but about placing it in the context of a life that is always moving forward, a life that is rich with opportunities for renewal and resilience.

Time, Pain, and Perspective

It's important to acknowledge that time alone is not a passive cure. Time works in tandem with your willingness to engage in healing - to reflect, to reframe, and to find meaning in the experience. As time moves forward, you can choose to view your pain not just as something that happened to you, but as something that can help you grow, evolve, and shape your understanding of yourself and the world.

This ability to reframe the meaning of our experiences is one of the most powerful aspects of Time-Based Reframing. When we look back on past difficulties, we often realize that what once felt unbearable has become a source of strength, a reminder of our capacity to endure. We begin to see the value in the lessons learned, the relationships that deepened, or the new paths we discovered in the aftermath of loss or trauma.

By leaning into the passage of time, you allow yourself to reclaim your narrative - to tell the story of your life not just through the lens of suffering, but through the lens of resilience, growth, and transformation. As time softens the sharp edges of your pain, it reveals the possibilities for healing and renewal that lie beyond the present moment.

Yet, even as time brings perspective, it also brings choice. One of the most empowering realizations you can have is that you get to choose what matters most. Not everything deserves your emotional investment, and not every battle is worth fighting. Time teaches us this as well - the realization that many of the things we once agonized over, many of the worries and fears that consumed us, were not as significant as they seemed at the time. As you look back, you can see the moments where you spent precious energy on things that, in hindsight, didn't truly matter.

This understanding naturally leads us to the next cognitive reframing approach: Select What Matters. While Time-Based Reframing helps you place your pain in the context of time and understand that healing is possible, Select What Matters invites you to take an even more active role in choosing what to care about, what to let go of, and where to focus your emotional energy.

Transitioning to Select What Matters: Focusing on What Truly Matters

As you begin to embrace the insights gained from Time-Based Reframing, the next natural step in the R.E.S.T. framework is Select What Matters. This phase is about focusing on what truly matters and letting go of the rest. While Time-Based Reframing helps you understand that emotions are fluid and time changes how we experience them, Select What Matters takes that wisdom a step further. It teaches us that not everything deserves our emotional investment or attention, especially in the face of trauma or hardship.

In moments of intense emotional overwhelm, it can feel like every detail of life demands your energy - every relationship, every expectation, every small failure or setback. But the truth is, we only have a limited amount of emotional and mental resources. When we invest those resources indiscriminately, we risk burnout, frustration, and a sense of being overwhelmed. Select What Matters is a powerful tool to cut through the noise and help you focus on what truly matters in the grand scheme of your life. It's about choosing what deserves your energy, and, just as importantly, what doesn't.

You might think of this step as the act of decluttering your mind and heart. You release the unnecessary concerns and trivial worries that do not serve your greater purpose or well-being, allowing you to focus your attention on the things that align with your deepest values. This doesn't mean embracing the negative connotations of nihilism, which often suggests that nothing in life matters. Instead, Select What Matters reframes this philosophy in a positive light: not everything matters, but some things deeply do. And your job is to discern which is which.

R.E.S.T. Practice

Applying Examine Through Time: Seeing Pain Beyond the Present Moment

This chapter helps you challenge the false permanence of trauma by viewing pain through time, distance, and future possibility.

Release: What needs to settle before you analyze this?

____

____

____

____

Examine Through Time: How might this feel or look different with time, distance, and support?

____

____

____

____

Select What Matters: What truly deserves your energy here?

____

____

____

____

Transform Meaning: What meaning can be built without minimizing what happened?

____

____

____

____

Reflection Prompts

- What pain am I treating as permanent because it feels intense today?

- How might I understand this from the perspective of my future self?

- What past experience reminds me that feelings can change over time?

Gentle Reminder

Do not force insight before your body has enough safety to hold it. Regulation comes before interpretation. You can return to any exercise slowly, briefly, and with support.

Daily Micro-Practice

Examine Through Time

Use this page as a brief daily practice. The point is repetition, not perfection. One honest sentence is enough.

Today I noticed:

____

____

____

____

The trauma-shaped story that appeared was:

____

____

____

____

The R.E.S.T. response I want to practice is:

____

____

____

____

One gentle action I can take next is:

____

____

____

____

Chapter 6

Select What Matters: Letting Go of What Trauma Taught You to Carry

Understanding Trauma and Emotional Overload

Before diving deeper into how Select What Matters can be applied, it's crucial to understand the profound psychological impact that trauma has on our priorities and thought processes. When we experience trauma, our brain's alarm systems go into overdrive. The amygdala - the part of the brain responsible for processing emotions like fear, anger, and anxiety - becomes hyperactive, perceiving every potential challenge or stressor as a threat. This overactive response is part of the brain's survival mechanism, designed to protect us from danger, but in the context of trauma, it can make even minor tasks feel overwhelming.

Meanwhile, the prefrontal cortex - the area responsible for rational decision-making, judgment, and assessing priorities - often becomes underactive. This imbalance between heightened emotional reactions and diminished cognitive control creates a situation where everything feels equally urgent, demanding, and critical. What were once simple tasks - answering a phone call, paying bills, or planning a day out - now feel monumental, as though they carry the weight of the world.

Trauma disrupts our sense of equilibrium, blurring the lines between what truly needs our attention and what can be let go. When every responsibility feels equally important, the resulting emotional state can lead to burnout, emotional exhaustion, and often a sense of paralysis, where we feel incapable of taking action or making decisions. We start to feel as though we're stuck in survival mode, constantly juggling the demands of life without a clear understanding of what deserves our energy.

This is where Select What Matters becomes a powerful tool, offering an antidote to this paralysis. By giving yourself permission to evaluate each task, thought, or emotional demand through a lens of importance, you can begin to reclaim agency over your life. You can start to differentiate between what genuinely requires your attention and what can be let go - whether temporarily or permanently. This process of evaluation is not about apathy; it's about making intentional decisions to prioritize what matters and release what doesn't contribute to your well-being and recovery.

Focusing on What Truly Matters

In today's world, we are constantly bombarded by distractions, pressures, and expectations - so much so that life can feel like a never-ending race. We live in a culture that glorifies busyness, productivity, and the constant pursuit of more. You're expected to excel at everything: your career, your relationships, your social image, and your personal development. There's a constant hum of voices - some external, some internal - telling you to work harder, look better, achieve more, be more.

And, quietly, beneath the surface, there's often an unspoken pressure to carry the emotional weight of all these demands, to shoulder the burdens of others while managing your own. As you try to keep up with these countless demands, you might find yourself feeling stretched too thin, struggling to breathe under the weight of it all. The result is a familiar, suffocating feeling: overwhelm, burnout, and emotional exhaustion.

We've all felt it. That moment when everything - every email, every task, every social obligation - feels equally important and equally deserving of your time and emotional energy. You may feel like you're constantly chasing an ideal version of yourself that's always just out of reach. As if you're running on a treadmill, trying to catch up, yet somehow always falling behind. Does this sound familiar?

But here's the truth: Not everything deserves your attention. Not every problem is yours to solve, not every expectation is yours to meet, and not every thought or emotion needs to be addressed with the same level of intensity. In fact, some things don't matter at all - and the sooner you recognize this, the freer and lighter your life becomes.

This is where Select What Matters steps in as a profoundly empowering and liberating philosophy. It offers you a clear and essential reminder: You don't have to care about everything. In fact, you shouldn't. Trying to give equal importance to every aspect of life -

whether it's work, social status, relationships, or even personal worries - is a sure path to emotional depletion. Select What Matters invites you to pause, reflect, and make a choice about where you direct your energy.

You have limited emotional, mental, and physical resources, and it's up to you to decide how you want to spend them. Not everything deserves your emotional investment, and realizing this is the first step toward regaining control over your inner life. When you stop trying to be everything to everyone, you make room for the things that truly matter to you - the things that align with your core values, bring you joy, and add meaning to your life.

This chapter will guide you through the philosophy behind Select What Matters, showing how it can help you reclaim your energy and create a more focused, intentional life. You'll learn practical ways to apply this approach, helping you to let go of what drains you and focus on what matters most.

Understanding Trauma and Emotional Overload: How Trauma Shifts Emotional Baselines

To fully appreciate the transformative power of Select What Matters and its application in life after trauma, it is essential to first understand how trauma fundamentally shifts our emotional baselines and alters our responses to everyday experiences. Trauma affects not just our emotional state in the moment, but also how we perceive, prioritize, and react to future stressors. This shift in emotional processing can make even the most mundane tasks feel insurmountable, distorting our sense of urgency and importance.

Trauma and the Brain: The Amygdala's Hyperactivity and the Prefrontal Cortex's Retreat

When we experience trauma, our brain's alarm systems go into overdrive. The amygdala, often referred to as the brain's "fear center," is responsible for processing emotions such as fear, anger, and anxiety. After trauma, this part of the brain becomes hyperactive, responding as though every stressor, no matter how minor, is a potential threat. The amygdala is designed to keep us safe by ensuring we react quickly to danger, but in the context of trauma, it begins to perceive everything - from a work deadline to a social interaction - as a source of danger or stress.

For example, after a traumatic event, even benign stimuli - a ringing phone, a knock at the door, or a comment made by a colleague - can trigger the amygdala's fight-or-flight response. Instead of assessing each situation logically, your brain jumps into action, flooding your body with stress hormones like cortisol and adrenaline. These hormones were designed to help us outrun a predator in ancient times, but in modern-day life, they manifest as feelings of anxiety, irritability, or even panic when faced with everyday challenges.

Simultaneously, trauma can impair the functioning of the prefrontal cortex, the area of the brain responsible for higher-level cognitive functions like judgment, rational decision-making, and impulse control. This is the part of the brain that helps us prioritize tasks, evaluate long-term consequences, and keep our emotions in check. After trauma, the prefrontal cortex becomes underactive, making it harder to process complex information or assess situations objectively. In this state, everything can feel equally urgent and overwhelming, contributing to emotional overload.

This imbalance between the hyperactive amygdala and the underactive prefrontal cortex is what makes trauma survivors more prone to feeling overwhelmed by even minor demands. It's not that everyday tasks have genuinely become more difficult; it's that the brain's ability to filter and prioritize them has been compromised. As a result, your emotional responses to situations that once felt manageable may now feel disproportionately intense.

The Emotional Recalibration After Trauma

Trauma also shifts our emotional baseline - the level at which we normally function day-to-day. Before trauma, we might have experienced stress or anxiety in response to significant life events, such as a job loss or a relationship breakup. However, after trauma, our baseline shifts, meaning we start from a place of heightened emotional arousal even during mundane tasks. The "default" emotional state for someone with trauma is often one of anxiety, hypervigilance, or emotional numbness, making it harder to experience moments of calm or neutrality.

Imagine your emotions on a scale from 1 to 10, where 1 represents complete relaxation and 10 represents full-blown panic. Before trauma, your baseline might have been around 3 or 4 - somewhere in the middle, where stressors would naturally push you higher on the scale, but you could return to a place of calm. After trauma, however, your baseline might shift to 7 or 8. This means that even small stressors - like an unexpected email or a delayed train - can push you straight into a state of emotional overload.

This recalibration of your emotional baseline means that your ability to cope with stress is reduced, not because you're incapable, but because your brain is operating from a heightened state of alertness. It's as if your nervous system is constantly in survival mode, scanning for threats, and unable to fully relax. This is why trauma survivors often report feeling "on edge" or as though they are waiting for the next disaster to strike, even when there is no immediate danger present.

Emotional Blurring: When Everything Feels Urgent

One of the most challenging effects of trauma on emotional responses is the way it blurs the lines between what truly requires our attention and what can be let go. Trauma survivors often experience what can be called "emotional blurring," where the brain's ability to differentiate between high-stakes situations and minor inconveniences becomes impaired. This means that every responsibility, interaction, or task can feel equally critical - whether it's an urgent work deadline or a simple decision about what to eat for dinner.

This emotional blurring can lead to a state of emotional paralysis, where we feel incapable of taking action because every decision feels overwhelming. It's as though every item on our mental to-do list is screaming for immediate attention, making it difficult to prioritize or assess which tasks actually need to be addressed. This sense of constant urgency can lead to burnout, where even minor responsibilities feel insurmountable because we've depleted our emotional reserves trying to manage everything at once.

The result is often a vicious cycle: the more overwhelmed you feel, the harder it becomes to make decisions, and the more likely you are to feel anxious about even the smallest tasks. Over time, this can lead to emotional exhaustion, where the weight of carrying all these demands leaves you feeling as though you're running on empty.

The Role of Select What Matters in Reclaiming Emotional Control

This is where Select What Matters becomes a powerful tool in trauma recovery. Select What Matters offers a way to cut through the emotional noise and reclaim agency over your priorities. It provides a framework for intentionally evaluating each thought, responsibility, or task, asking whether it truly deserves your emotional investment. By practicing Select What Matters, you allow yourself to step back from the emotional blurring caused by trauma and differentiate between what requires your attention and what can be released.

It's important to clarify that Select What Matters is not about ignoring responsibilities or becoming indifferent to life's challenges. Instead, it's about recognizing that you have limited emotional, mental, and physical resources, and you must choose carefully how you spend them. It's about understanding that not every situation, task, or relationship is worth your emotional energy, especially when that energy is already depleted from the impact of trauma.

By embracing Select What Matters, you give yourself permission to let go of the things that don't truly matter, creating space for healing, self-care, and meaningful connections. This process of letting go is especially important for trauma survivors because it helps recalibrate your emotional responses, bringing you back into balance by reducing unnecessary stress and freeing up emotional bandwidth for what truly matters.

How Trauma Distorts Our Sense of Self and Responsibility

In addition to shifting emotional baselines and priorities, trauma can also distort our sense of self and responsibility. Many trauma survivors internalize a belief that they are responsible for everything and everyone around them. This can manifest in feelings of guilt, shame, or a constant need to fix problems that aren't theirs to solve.

For instance, trauma survivors might feel responsible for managing other people's emotions, taking on more work than they can handle, or maintaining relationships that no longer serve them out of a sense of obligation. This hyper-responsibility is often a survival mechanism that develops during or after trauma, as the brain attempts to exert control over an uncontrollable situation. However, in the long term, this need to manage everything only contributes to emotional burnout and reinforces the feeling of being overwhelmed.

Select What Matters can help break this cycle by encouraging you to recognize what is - and is not - within your control. It invites you to release the burdens of others' expectations and to prioritize your own well-being without feeling guilty. This is especially important in trauma recovery, where survivors often struggle with feelings of unworthiness or the belief that their needs are less important than those of others.

Living in a World That Demands Too Much

We live in an age of constant stimulation. Whether it's the relentless pinging of notifications, the avalanche of news and opinions on social media, or the unspoken pressure to keep up with the latest trends, there's always something vying for your attention. Everywhere you turn, it feels like there's something demanding you to care about it, to respond, to engage. And this bombardment comes not only from the outside world but from the internal pressure we place on ourselves - the belief that we must be productive, that we must excel at everything, that we must be always "on."

But this constant, high-stakes approach to life is unsustainable. We try to juggle careers, personal lives, family obligations, and the expectations of our peers, all while managing the subtle yet weighty burden of feeling like we must be "enough" in every area. It's as though society hands us an endless list of tasks and responsibilities, expecting us to complete them all with grace and perfection.

It's no wonder, then, that so many of us feel overwhelmed and disconnected from ourselves. When everything feels equally important, when every moment feels like a test of your worth, you start to lose touch with what really matters. You begin to treat even the smallest, most trivial concerns with the same level of intensity as the truly important ones.

Think about how often you've found yourself worrying about things that don't really matter in the grand scheme of your life. Maybe you've spent sleepless nights agonizing over a social interaction - a comment someone made that seemed critical or a glance that you interpreted as judgment. Or perhaps you've found yourself feeling pressured to meet societal standards that don't align with your values, such as striving for material success or maintaining a certain image on social media.

In moments like these, it's easy to feel like you must care about everything, that everything demands your emotional investment. But the reality is, not everything is equally important. Some of the things that consume your thoughts, that make you feel anxious or inadequate, are simply not worth your time or energy.

Select What Matters encourages you to challenge this assumption. It invites you to step back from the constant rush of life and ask yourself a simple yet profound question: "Does this truly matter?" Does this worry, this expectation, this external pressure align with your core values? Is it worth the emotional energy you're giving it?

The Liberation of Letting Go

One of the most liberating aspects of Select What Matters is the realization that you don't have to care about everything. In fact, it's essential to let go of the things that don't serve you, that don't contribute to your well-being or happiness. This doesn't mean you adopt a cold, detached attitude toward life or give up on responsibility. Instead, Select What Matters is about making a deliberate choice: where are you going to invest your limited emotional resources?

Think about the emotional baggage we all carry - petty conflicts, societal expectations, toxic relationships, the pressure to live up to others' standards. These things drain our energy and take up valuable mental space, leaving us exhausted and disconnected from what really matters. Select What Matters asks you to release this baggage. It's about giving yourself permission to say, "I don't need to care about this. This isn't my burden to carry."

By doing so, you begin to reclaim your emotional freedom. You no longer feel the weight of having to fix every problem, meet every expectation, or invest in every superficial concern. Instead, you create space for the things that truly bring you joy, fulfillment, and meaning.

This practice of letting go is a form of emotional decluttering. Just as you might declutter your physical environment by getting rid of things you no longer need, Select What Matters encourages you to declutter your internal world. You let go of the beliefs, expectations, and worries that weigh you down, making room for what truly matters.

The Power of Emotional Prioritization

At its core, Select What Matters is about emotional prioritization. Just as you would prioritize tasks on a to-do list, you can also prioritize where to direct your emotional energy. Not everything deserves the same level of investment, and by acknowledging this, you take a significant step toward living with greater clarity and intention.

When you practice Select What Matters, you're not abandoning your responsibilities or disengaging from life. Instead, you're making an intentional decision to focus on what's most meaningful to you. You're choosing to invest your emotional resources where they count - on the relationships, passions, and experiences that truly align with your values.

For example, imagine how often we waste emotional energy on things that don't matter in the long run - worrying about what others think, feeling guilty about not being perfect, stressing over small inconveniences. By shifting your focus away from these distractions and toward the things that enrich your life, you simplify your emotional world. You stop wasting energy on things that don't serve you and redirect that energy toward what does.

Select What Matters gives you the freedom to say, "I choose to care about these things, and I choose to let go of the rest." This act of prioritization helps you live with a greater sense of peace and balance. You're no longer pulled in a hundred different directions by societal pressures or internal expectations. Instead, you're anchored in what truly matters to you.

How Select What Matters Works: Simplifying Your Internal World

So how do you put Select What Matters into practice? How do you actually apply this philosophy to your daily life in a way that feels meaningful and empowering?

The first step is recognizing that you can't control everything. Life is full of unpredictable challenges, external expectations, and societal pressures that are often beyond your control. Trying to micromanage every part of your life, or feeling responsible for everyone's opinions or expectations, is a recipe for burnout. When you spread yourself too thin, you end up investing emotional energy into things that don't truly matter, leaving you exhausted and unfulfilled.

Select What Matters helps you cut through this clutter by forcing you to ask the tough, yet essential, question: "Does this really matter in the grand scheme of my life?"

Let's break down how Select What Matters works in practice:

1. Identify the Emotional Drains in Your Life

The first step toward practicing Select What Matters is identifying where your emotional energy is being spent unnecessarily. This requires taking an honest look at the things in your life that consume your mental and emotional resources without giving much back in return. These can be worries, obligations, or expectations that you feel pressured to meet, even though they don't align with your values or your long-term vision.

For example, are you constantly worrying about what others think of you? Do you find yourself feeling obligated to attend social events out of fear of missing out or disappointing someone? Are you pouring emotional energy into trying to achieve a level of success that doesn't actually align with your personal goals but is driven by societal norms?

When you begin to recognize these emotional drains, you give yourself the opportunity to question whether they deserve your energy in the first place.

Ask yourself:

What am I stressing about that doesn't actually matter long-term?

Am I investing energy in things that align with my core values?

What am I holding onto simply because of external pressure, not because it genuinely matters to me?

By identifying these emotional drains, you can begin to sort through what is truly important and what isn't.

2. Define What Truly Matters

Once you've identified where you're wasting emotional energy, the next step is to clarify what really matters to you. These are the things that bring meaning, fulfillment, and joy to your life. This could be your relationships, your creative passions, your personal growth, or your connection to your inner purpose.

The challenge here is that we often lose sight of what truly matters because we're so caught up in daily distractions and societal pressures. We spend our days chasing what we think we should care about, rather than reflecting on what genuinely aligns with our values.

Take some time to ask yourself:

What do I genuinely care about?

What brings me joy, peace, and fulfillment?

What aligns with my long-term vision for myself and my life?

This step is about becoming clear on your core values. Once you know what these are, you can make more intentional choices about where to direct your energy, and Select What Matters becomes a tool for simplifying your internal world. You stop wasting time and emotional bandwidth on things that don't contribute to your growth, and you start focusing on the people, experiences, and pursuits that truly enrich your life.

3. Let Go of the Rest

This step, while often the most difficult, is also the most liberating: letting go of the things that don't truly matter. It's about releasing the need to care about every little detail, every opinion, and every expectation that others impose on you.

Think of it as an act of emotional decluttering. Just as you would clean out a messy room by getting rid of items you no longer need, Select What Matters encourages you to declutter your emotional and mental space by letting go of the things that no longer serve you. These could be relationships that drain you, societal pressures that don't align with your values, or expectations that keep you trapped in a cycle of overthinking.

When you let go, you create more room for what's meaningful. Select What Matters teaches you to say, "This is not my burden to carry," and in doing so, you free yourself from the emotional weight that's been holding you down.

Letting go might mean:

No longer worrying about others' opinions of your life choices.

Choosing to release toxic relationships that drain your energy.

Deciding that you don't need to pursue external markers of success that don't resonate with your personal values.

Setting boundaries around what demands your time and attention.

The practice of letting go allows you to focus on what genuinely matters, giving you a sense of emotional freedom and control over your internal world. It's not about being careless or detached, but rather about being intentional about where you invest your energy.

The Benefits of Select What Matters

When you embrace Select What Matters, the transformation in your life can be profound. By making conscious choices about where to direct your emotional energy, you create space for a more intentional, fulfilling existence. Here are some of the key benefits:

1. Emotional Freedom: Breaking the Chains of Expectations

One of the most immediate benefits of Select What Matters is the sense of emotional freedom it offers. By letting go of the things that don't matter, you free yourself from the expectations, pressures, and anxieties that once weighed you down. You no longer feel obligated to meet every expectation or worry about what others think.

This emotional freedom allows you to focus on what aligns with your values and goals, leading to a more authentic and empowered life. You stop carrying the emotional baggage that doesn't belong to you and instead focus on building a life that reflects who you truly are.

Imagine how much lighter you'd feel if you no longer worried about pleasing everyone or meeting society's constantly shifting standards of success. Imagine the peace that comes from knowing that you get to decide what's important in your life. This is the freedom that Select What Matters brings.

2. Clarity and Focus: Simplifying Your Life

When you practice Select What Matters, you develop a clearer sense of what truly matters. You begin to filter out the distractions and noise of everyday life, allowing you to focus on what brings you meaning and joy. This clarity leads to a more intentional and purposeful existence, where your decisions are aligned with your values and long-term goals.

With this newfound clarity, you'll find that your life becomes simpler. You no longer feel the need to juggle a thousand competing demands, and instead, you can focus on the few things that truly matter to you. This simplification not only reduces stress but also allows you to be more present and engaged in the moments that count.

3. Reduced Stress and Anxiety: Letting Go of the Non-Essential

Many of the stressors we experience in life are the result of feeling like we have to care about everything. We worry about what others think, we stress over achieving arbitrary goals, and we feel anxious about things beyond our control. Select What Matters teaches you that not everything deserves your worry. When you choose to focus only on what truly matters, your stress levels naturally decrease.

By letting go of the non-essential, you create more space for calm and peace in your life. You stop feeling like you're constantly running to catch up and instead move through life with greater ease, knowing that you're focusing on the right things.

4. Stronger, More Fulfilling Relationships

When you practice Select What Matters, you also begin to refine your relationships. You let go of relationships that drain your energy or don't align with your values, and you focus on nurturing the connections that bring you joy and support. This leads to deeper, more fulfilling relationships, as you invest your time and emotional energy into people who truly matter to you.

By surrounding yourself with relationships that nourish you, you create a supportive and loving community that aligns with your values. Select What Matters allows you to cultivate relationships that enhance your life rather than deplete it.

Sarah's Journey with Select What Matters

In the R.E.S.T. framework, we now reach an essential turning point: Select What Matters. This step is where you stop giving your emotional energy to everything that crosses your path and start focusing only on what truly matters. It's about creating space in your life for what aligns with your deepest values and letting go of what drains you. In this chapter, we'll continue following Sarah's journey, as she transitions from the Release and Time-Based Reframing phases to embrace Select What Matters and reclaim her emotional freedom.

Living in a World That Demands Too Much

Sarah, now several months into her recovery journey following the traumatic car accident, has begun to experience more emotional distance from the event. Thanks to her practice of grounding techniques, deep breathing, and Time-Based Reframing, she no longer feels the same level of panic every time she sees the intersection where the accident occurred. With time, she's also been able to shift her perspective on the accident, seeing it not as the defining moment of her life but as one event among many, from which she can grow and learn.

Yet, Sarah still feels emotionally drained in other areas of her life. Since the accident, she has taken on the role of the "strong one" in her family, always being there for her kids, trying to maintain a perfect home, and never showing her vulnerability. Additionally, she's feeling overwhelmed at work, where she's constantly pushing herself to make up for the time she took off after the accident. On top of all this, her friends have started pressuring her to return to her old social self - someone who was always there for others, hosting gatherings and planning nights out.

Although she has made progress in healing from the trauma, Sarah feels like she's drowning in expectations - both from others and from herself. Every day feels like a balancing act, trying to meet everyone's needs while ignoring her own exhaustion. She knows she's spread too thin, but she doesn't know how to stop caring about everything or how to prioritize what really matters.

This is where Select What Matters enters the picture. It teaches Sarah that not every task, obligation, or expectation deserves her emotional investment. In fact, many of the pressures she feels are things she can let go of - societal expectations, the need to be perfect, and the constant worrying about pleasing others.

Understanding Emotional Overload

Sarah's experience of emotional overload is something many of us can relate to. We live in a world where we're constantly bombarded by demands, expectations, and pressures from every direction. Whether it's at work, at home, in social situations, or even online, there's a relentless pressure to do more, be more, and care about everything. The problem is, trying to give equal attention and care to everything leads to burnout.

For Sarah, these pressures have come in different forms. At work, she feels the need to prove that her accident hasn't slowed her down, so she's overloading herself with extra projects. At home, she feels like she has to keep it all together for her children, maintaining the illusion of perfection, never showing weakness. With her friends, she feels the unspoken pressure to return to being the life of the party - something that no longer feels aligned with who she is after the accident.

It's a classic example of emotional overload. When everything feels equally important, when every expectation feels like a priority, it's easy to lose sight of what really matters.

This is where Select What Matters offers Sarah a lifeline. It gives her the permission to step back and ask, "Does this really matter?" "Is this worth my emotional energy?" and "Am I carrying burdens that aren't mine to carry?".

The Liberation of Letting Go

One of the most empowering aspects of Select What Matters is realizing that not everything deserves your emotional investment. You don't have to care about every expectation, fix every problem, or meet every demand. In fact, you shouldn't. Letting go of the things that don't align with your core values is the first step toward reclaiming your emotional freedom.

For Sarah, this realization was both a relief and a challenge. She had spent so much time trying to be everything to everyone that she didn't know how to stop. She worried that if she let go of certain responsibilities, things would fall apart - at home, at work, and in her relationships. But through Select What Matters, Sarah learned that letting go doesn't mean abandoning your responsibilities or disengaging from life. Instead, it means making deliberate choices about where you invest your energy.

The truth is, emotional energy is finite. Just like your time and physical energy, you can only give so much before you're depleted. By continuing to invest in the things that don't truly matter, you drain your emotional resources, leaving little for what does matter - your own well-being, meaningful relationships, and personal growth.

Applying Select What Matters to Sarah's Life

Sarah's first step in applying Select What Matters was to identify where she was spending emotional energy unnecessarily. She began to reflect on the parts of her life that were draining her, asking herself, "Is this something I genuinely care about, or am I just doing it out of obligation?"

1. Work Pressures

At work, Sarah realized that much of her stress came from her belief that she had to prove herself. She had been pushing herself to overperform, taking on extra projects to show that she was still the same high-achiever she was before the accident. But was that truly necessary? Did it align with her values?

After reflecting on it, Sarah realized that much of this pressure was self-imposed. She was operating from a place of fear - fear that her colleagues might think less of her, fear that she wasn't capable anymore. But when she examined these fears through the lens of Select What Matters, she realized that her need to prove herself didn't truly matter. What mattered to Sarah was doing meaningful work and finding balance in her life.

With this realization , Sarah made a conscious decision to let go of the need to overperform at work. She spoke to her manager about adjusting her workload to a more sustainable level and set boundaries around her working hours. Instead of staying late or taking on unnecessary projects, Sarah focused on completing her core responsibilities with care and quality. By doing so, she was able to reduce her stress and emotional exhaustion, giving her more energy for other areas of her life that truly mattered.

2. Social Expectations

Sarah also took a hard look at her social life. Before the accident, she had been the one to organize outings, host gatherings, and keep in touch with a wide circle of friends. After the accident, however, socializing felt overwhelming. Her friends, though well-meaning, expected her to return to her previous role as the "planner" of the group. Sarah felt guilty for not being able to keep up, but she also knew that she simply didn't have the energy for it anymore.

Using the principles of Select What Matters, Sarah asked herself: "Does maintaining this level of social activity truly align with my values and current needs?" The answer was no. She valued meaningful connections, but she didn't need to be involved in every social event to maintain those connections.

Sarah decided to let go of the pressure to be constantly available to her friends. She realized that her true friendships would survive without her always being the one to organize things. So, she stepped back from the social obligations that didn't fulfill her, and instead focused on nurturing a few close relationships that brought her joy and emotional support. This shift allowed Sarah to be more present in her friendships without feeling overextended.

3. Perfectionism at Home

At home, Sarah was holding herself to an impossible standard of perfection. She felt that as a mother, she needed to always appear strong, capable, and unfazed by her own struggles. She worried that if she showed vulnerability, her children might feel unsafe or insecure. As a result, she was constantly pushing herself to maintain a spotless house, make perfect meals, and never let her children see her cry or express frustration.

But was this constant pursuit of perfection necessary? Did it actually serve her family, or was it adding unnecessary pressure to her life?

Through Select What Matters, Sarah began to question her perfectionism. She realized that her children didn't need her to be perfect - they needed her to be present and emotionally available. The stress she was putting on herself to maintain an unrealistic image of perfection was draining her, and it wasn't truly benefiting her family.

So, Sarah let go of the need to be a "perfect" mom. She allowed herself to show vulnerability in front of her children, explaining that it was okay to feel sad or frustrated sometimes. She also relaxed her standards around household tasks, recognizing that it was more important to spend quality time with her kids than to have a spotless home. This shift not only eased her own emotional burden but also strengthened her connection with her children, who felt more comfortable expressing their own emotions.

The Power of Emotional Prioritization

At its core, Select What Matters is about emotional prioritization - choosing where to focus your emotional energy and letting go of what doesn't align with your values or serve your well-being. By embracing this approach, Sarah was able to reclaim her emotional freedom and simplify her life.

Instead of trying to be everything to everyone, Sarah learned to prioritize what truly mattered to her: being a present and emotionally available mother, maintaining meaningful friendships, and finding balance in her work. Everything else - her need to prove herself, her perfectionism, and her social obligations - was no longer worthy of her emotional investment.

This shift in focus allowed Sarah to live with greater clarity and intention. She no longer felt pulled in a hundred different directions by external pressures or internal expectations. Instead, she was anchored in what truly mattered, and that gave her a sense of peace and emotional balance that she hadn't experienced in a long time.

Letting Go: The Key to Emotional Freedom

Letting go of the things that don't matter is one of the most challenging but liberating aspects of Select What Matters. For Sarah, this meant releasing the guilt she felt for not being everything to everyone. It meant accepting that she couldn't meet every expectation - at work, at home, or in her social life - and that she didn't need to.

By letting go, Sarah created space in her life for what truly mattered. She stopped wasting emotional energy on the things that drained her, and she redirected that energy toward the people, experiences, and pursuits that enriched her life.

This wasn't easy. Letting go of perfectionism, social pressures, and self-imposed expectations can feel like a loss at first. But in reality, it's a gain - a gain of emotional freedom, clarity, and the ability to live in alignment with your core values.

The Benefits of Select What Matters in Sarah's Life

Sarah's journey through Select What Matters brought profound changes to her life. By focusing on what truly mattered, she experienced several key benefits:

Emotional Freedom: Sarah no longer felt weighed down by the need to be everything to everyone. She let go of the societal and self-imposed expectations that had been draining her. This gave her the freedom to focus on what aligned with her values and brought her joy.

Clarity and Focus: By simplifying her life and focusing on what mattered most, Sarah gained a clearer sense of purpose. She stopped worrying about what didn't matter and directed her energy toward the things that truly enriched her life, such as her relationships with her children and her close friends.

Reduced Stress and Anxiety: Letting go of the non-essential allowed Sarah to reduce her stress levels significantly. She no longer felt the constant pressure to prove herself at work or maintain an image of perfection at home. Instead, she embraced a more balanced, realistic approach to life.

Stronger Relationships: By focusing on nurturing her most meaningful relationships and letting go of superficial social obligations, Sarah was able to deepen her connections with the people who truly mattered to her. This brought more fulfillment and emotional support into her life.

Applying Select What Matters in Your Own Life

Just like Sarah, you can use Select What Matters to reclaim your emotional energy and create a more focused, intentional life. The key is to start by identifying where you're spending emotional energy unnecessarily, define what truly matters to you, and let go of the rest.

Ask yourself:

What am I stressing about that doesn't actually matter long-term?

Am I investing energy in things that align with my core values?

What am I holding onto simply because of external pressure, not because it genuinely matters to me?

Once you've identified the emotional drains in your life, begin the process of letting go. Release the need to care about everything. It's not about being detached or indifferent - it's about being intentional with your emotional resources. Choose to care deeply about the things that align with your values and bring you fulfillment, and let go of the rest.

By doing this, you'll experience the same emotional freedom, clarity, and reduced stress that Sarah did. You'll be able to focus on what truly matters in your life and create space for more joy, meaning, and peace.

In the next chapter, we'll explore the final phase of the R.E.S.T. framework: Transform Meaning. This phase will guide you in finding deep, personal meaning in your experiences, helping you to integrate your trauma into a larger narrative of growth and transformation.

R.E.S.T. Practice

Applying Select What Matters: Letting Go of What Trauma Taught You to Carry

This chapter helps you separate what deserves your energy from what trauma, guilt, fear, or pressure taught you to carry.

Release: What needs to settle before you analyze this?

____

____

____

____

Examine Through Time: How might this feel or look different with time, distance, and support?

____

____

____

____

Select What Matters: What truly deserves your energy here?

____

____

____

____

Transform Meaning: What meaning can be built without minimizing what happened?

____

____

____

____

Reflection Prompts

- What am I carrying that does not truly belong to me?

- What values deserve more of my emotional energy?

- What expectation, guilt, or fear am I ready to set down?

Gentle Reminder

Do not force insight before your body has enough safety to hold it. Regulation comes before interpretation. You can return to any exercise slowly, briefly, and with support.

Daily Micro-Practice

Select What Matters

Use this page as a brief daily practice. The point is repetition, not perfection. One honest sentence is enough.

Today I noticed:

____

____

____

____

The trauma-shaped story that appeared was:

____

____

____

____

The R.E.S.T. response I want to practice is:

____

____

____

____

One gentle action I can take next is:

____

____

____

____

Chapter 7

Transform Meaning: Building a Life Beyond What Happened

Turning Trauma into Purpose

In the final phase of the R.E.S.T. framework, we step into the deepest, most transformative realm: Transform Meaning. Trauma has a way of shaking us to our core. It disrupts not only our sense of safety but also our understanding of life itself. In the wake of trauma, we often find ourselves grappling with questions that cut to the heart of our existence: Why did this happen to me? What is the point of all this pain? What does it mean for my future, my identity, my purpose?

These are not easy questions. Trauma often forces us into an existential crisis, leaving us questioning everything we once believed about ourselves and the world. It strips away the illusions of control and certainty, exposing the raw truth of life's unpredictability. But within this crisis lies the potential for profound transformation. If we allow ourselves to fully engage with the questions trauma presents, we can emerge not just as survivors, but as people who have been reshaped and strengthened by our experiences.

In this phase, Transform Meaning invites us to explore how trauma can become a source of deep personal growth. It's about finding a way to make sense of the suffering - not by erasing it or minimizing it, but by integrating it into a broader understanding of our lives. By discovering meaning in our trauma, we begin to reclaim our narrative, turning moments of pain into catalysts for purpose, wisdom, and a renewed connection to what truly matters.

The Existential Crisis: When Trauma Shakes Our Foundation

Trauma often brings with it an existential reckoning. The life we knew, the plans we had, and the person we thought we were can all feel shattered in the aftermath. We find ourselves standing in the ruins of our old life, unsure of how to rebuild or even if rebuilding is possible.

It's in these moments that we're confronted with the big questions: Why did this happen? What am I supposed to do now? What does this mean for my future? These questions can be terrifying, because they force us to confront the unknown. Trauma takes away the comfort of certainty, and we're left to grapple with life's unpredictability.

But this existential crisis, as painful as it is, also offers an opportunity. It's a moment where we're invited to redefine ourselves, to ask not just what we've lost, but what we can gain. This is where the journey toward meaning transformation begins - by choosing to see trauma not as an end, but as a turning point.

Finding Meaning in Suffering: A New Narrative

Transform Meaning teaches us that while we cannot always control the events in our lives, we can control the narrative we build around them. Trauma can feel like an unwelcome intruder, upending everything we thought we knew. But what if we stopped seeing trauma as something that happens to us and started seeing it as something that happens through us? What if our pain became not a burden but a pathway to deeper understanding and purpose?

This shift in perspective doesn't happen overnight. It's a process - one that requires us to sit with our pain, to examine it, and to allow it to reshape us. But when we begin to see our suffering as something that can teach us, rather than something that simply takes from us, we open the door to new possibilities.

The key to this transformation lies in reframing the questions we ask ourselves. Instead of Why me?, we ask: What now? What can I learn from this? How can this experience deepen my understanding of life? These questions don't diminish the pain - they honor it by turning it into a source of insight and strength.

Finding Meaning

In life, suffering is not only unavoidable - it's inevitable. No matter how carefully we try to protect ourselves or our loved ones, adversity, in its many forms - loss, trauma, grief, or pain - finds its way to us. The human condition is marked by this inescapable truth. Yet, it's not the presence of suffering itself that defines us. Instead, it is the way we engage with and respond to our suffering that profoundly shapes who we become. For some, suffering leads to a downward spiral into despair - a sense of hopelessness that can overwhelm, paralyze, and seemingly define their existence. But for others, suffering becomes a source of deep transformation - a crucible through which resilience, wisdom, and meaning are forged.

This idea lies at the heart of Logotherapy, a therapeutic approach developed by the renowned psychiatrist Viktor Frankl, who survived unimaginable horrors during his imprisonment in Nazi concentration camps. Frankl observed that those who managed to survive the grueling and dehumanizing conditions often shared one critical trait: they were able to find meaning in their suffering. It wasn't the strongest or the most physically capable who endured, but those who could attach a sense of purpose to their suffering. From this observation, Frankl developed Logotherapy, a school of thought that asserts the primary drive in human beings is not the pursuit of pleasure or power, as some psychologists have suggested, but the pursuit of meaning - even in the darkest and most challenging circumstances.

The Search for Meaning as a Survival Mechanism

Frankl's experiences during the Holocaust gave him unique insight into the human spirit's capacity to transcend suffering through the search for meaning. In the camps, he witnessed firsthand how those who could find a sense of purpose - no matter how small - were often the ones who managed to maintain their humanity, their dignity, and ultimately their will to live. Whether it was the hope of reuniting with a loved one, the desire to finish a creative project, or the belief that their suffering would serve a greater cause, these survivors found a reason to keep going.

The core philosophy of Logotherapy rests on the idea that suffering, while painful and often devastating, can be reframed into something purposeful. We may not be able to control the circumstances of our suffering - whether it's a traumatic event, a loss, or a life-altering diagnosis - but we do have the power to choose how we respond to it. In choosing our response, we reclaim agency over our lives and begin the process of transforming suffering from a destructive force into one that builds resilience, growth, and strength.

This reframing of suffering doesn't come easily. In the midst of trauma, it's natural to ask, "Why me?" and to feel that the world is unjust or indifferent to our pain. But Logotherapy invites us to shift the question from "Why me?" to "What can I learn from this?" or "How can I use this experience to shape my life in a meaningful way?" It is in this reframing that suffering is transformed into something that strengthens rather than breaks us.

The Essence of Logotherapy: The Freedom to Choose Our Response

One of the central tenets of Logotherapy is that while we cannot always control what happens to us, we can always control how we respond. Frankl often spoke of this freedom as the "last of the human freedoms" - the ability to choose one's attitude in any given set of circumstances. This freedom is not dependent on external conditions but on our internal capacity to find meaning in even the most painful experiences.

Frankl's philosophy emphasizes that suffering, while unavoidable, does not need to be purposeless. It can be a powerful catalyst for growth and self-discovery if we allow ourselves to engage with it in a meaningful way. Instead of simply enduring pain, we can actively search for the lessons it has to offer. In doing so, we reclaim a sense of agency, turning what could have been a purely destructive experience into an opportunity for transformation.

In essence, Logotherapy teaches that suffering is not what breaks us - what breaks us is the belief that our suffering is meaningless. When we lose sight of meaning, we lose the will to continue. But when we can find even a glimmer of purpose, we tap into a deep well of resilience. This resilience allows us to move beyond the pain, not by escaping it, but by integrating it into the larger story of our lives.

Reframing Suffering: Shifting from "Why Me?" to "What Now?"

The path to finding meaning in suffering begins with a critical shift in perspective. Instead of focusing on the injustice or randomness of the pain we're experiencing, we begin to ask different questions. What can I learn from this? How can this experience deepen my understanding of myself or others? What values or strengths have been revealed through this challenge?

This shift from victimhood to agency is the essence of what Frankl described as the "tragic optimism" - the ability to maintain hope and find meaning even in the face of tragedy. It's not about denying the pain or pretending that everything happens for a reason. Instead, it's about acknowledging the reality of the suffering while choosing to search for meaning in the midst of it.

This shift doesn't mean that the suffering itself becomes "good." Rather, it means that we choose to make something good come out of it. The suffering becomes a crucible in which our character is tested, and through this process, we discover parts of ourselves we might never have known existed - our strength, our resilience, our capacity for empathy and love.

Suffering as a Gateway to Purpose

Through Logotherapy, Frankl reminds us that life's meaning is not always found in the absence of suffering but often in how we respond to it. This perspective encourages us to see suffering as a potential gateway to discovering or deepening our sense of purpose. When we reframe suffering in this way, we open ourselves to the possibility of growth and transformation.

For example, many people who have experienced profound trauma or loss go on to become advocates, healers, or educators in areas directly related to their suffering. A person who has survived cancer might find purpose in supporting others through their treatment. Someone who has lost a loved one to addiction may dedicate their life to raising awareness about substance abuse. These individuals have not erased their suffering, but they have integrated it into their lives in a way that brings purpose and meaning to both themselves and others.

This doesn't mean that every traumatic experience needs to result in a life of advocacy or public action. Meaning can be found in quieter ways as well - in the deepening of relationships, in the cultivation of empathy, or in a renewed commitment to living in alignment with one's values. What's important is that the suffering is not wasted. It is transformed into something that adds value to our lives and the lives of those around us.

The Journey Toward Meaning: A Lifelong Process

Finding meaning in suffering is not a one-time achievement. It is a lifelong process, one that evolves as we grow and change. The meaning we derive from our suffering may shift over time as we gain new insights and experiences. What matters is that we continue to engage with the process, remaining open to the lessons that our pain has to offer.

Logotherapy teaches us that life's meaning is not static; it is something we must continually seek and redefine. This process of meaning-making is what gives life its richness and depth. It allows us to move through our suffering with a sense of purpose and direction, rather than feeling lost or adrift.

In the end, suffering is a part of the human experience. But it does not need to be the defining feature of our lives. Through Logotherapy, we learn that while we may not choose our suffering, we can choose how we respond to it. And in that choice lies the power to transform our pain into something meaningful - something that strengthens us, deepens our relationships, and connects us to the greater purpose of our lives.

Suffering as a Path to Meaning

Viktor Frankl's Logotherapy offers a profound reminder that suffering, while painful, is not without purpose. It challenges us to look beyond the immediate pain and ask how we can use our experiences to shape a life of deeper meaning, connection, and purpose. By shifting our perspective from Why me? to What now?, we reclaim our power to write our own narrative, transforming our suffering into a source of strength and wisdom.

In the end, it is not the absence of suffering that makes life meaningful, but our ability to find purpose within it. Suffering, when reframed through the lens of meaning, becomes not a burden, but a stepping stone on the path to greater understanding and growth. Through this process, we not only survive - we thrive.

Reframing Suffering

At the heart of Logotherapy is the idea that suffering, when viewed through the right lens, can become a source of personal growth and purpose. This approach doesn't seek to diminish or erase pain but instead helps you reinterpret it within the broader context of your life. Through Logotherapy, you learn to see hardship not as the enemy, but as a teacher, guiding you toward a deeper understanding of yourself and the world around you.

Frankl famously said, "When we are no longer able to change a situation, we are challenged to change ourselves." This is the essence of the Logotherapeutic approach - shifting our perspective from what has been lost to what can still be gained, from suffering as a destructive force to suffering as a path to greater meaning.

But how do we begin this process of reframing suffering? How do we start to find meaning when we feel consumed by pain?

The Cognitive Reframing Exercise: Re-examining the Totality of Your Life

In our journey toward healing and finding meaning in suffering, Logotherapy offers us an essential, transformative tool: the ability to step back from the immediate pain of trauma and see our lives through a broader, more expansive lens. Trauma, while intense and often all-consuming in the moment, can distort our perception of our overall existence. It can make us feel as though our entire lives are defined by suffering, obscuring the neutral and positive experiences that have also shaped who we are.

To help you navigate this reframing process, this cognitive reframing exercise invites you to map out your life in its totality, reflecting on the vast landscape of your lived experiences. By examining your memories - both painful and joyful, major and minor - you can begin to place your trauma in proportion to the entirety of your life. The goal is to help you see that while trauma is significant, it is only one chapter in the much larger story of your existence.

The Purpose of the Exercise

Why does trauma seem to dominate our memories so intensely? This happens because of a phenomenon known as cognitive distortion. Our brains are wired to focus on emotionally intense experiences, particularly negative ones, which demand more of our attention and leave deeper imprints on our memory. When we endure trauma, it often takes on an outsized presence in our minds, overshadowing other life events. This can create a distorted view of our lives, where the suffering feels as though it defines everything.

The purpose of this exercise is to help you recontextualize your trauma within the broader scope of your entire life. By reflecting on how much of your life has been neutral or even positive, you can begin to loosen the grip that trauma holds over your identity. Trauma, while impactful, is only one of many experiences that have shaped who you are. It is not the whole story.

This exercise is transformative because it allows you to take a step back from your immediate emotional experience and see your life through a wider, more balanced perspective. It helps you realize that while trauma may feel overwhelming, it does not define your existence. Instead, it becomes one part of a rich and complex life filled with other moments that are equally, if not more, important.

Steps to Perform the Exercise

This exercise is not meant to be done quickly; it requires patience, self-reflection, and a willingness to explore the full spectrum of your memories. The goal is not perfection but discovery - to uncover insights about how your trauma fits into the larger context of your life. Here are the steps to guide you through this process:

1. Set Aside Uninterrupted Time

To fully engage in this exercise, find a quiet, comfortable space where you can focus without distractions. Set aside at least an hour of uninterrupted time. Turn off your phone, close the door, and give yourself the freedom to be alone with your thoughts. Creating this space is essential, as it allows you to dive deeply into your memories without the external world pulling you away.

Approach the exercise with an open heart and mind. Remind yourself that this is a time for reflection and exploration, not judgment or pressure.

2. Begin by Recalling Your Earliest Memory

Start by reaching back to your earliest memory - no matter how vague, fragmented, or incomplete it may seem. Write down whatever comes to mind, even if it feels insignificant. This memory could be a happy childhood moment, like playing outside or holding a favorite toy, or a neutral experience, like sitting in a classroom or walking down a street. It could also be a confusing or emotional event, such as your first encounter with fear or loneliness.

The key is to begin with the first moment you can access. This memory will serve as your starting point, anchoring you as you journey through the unfolding narrative of your life.

3. Write Out Your Life, Moment by Moment

From this initial memory, start to retrace the steps of your life, allowing each memory to flow into the next. As you recall different moments, write them down - don't worry about creating a perfect, linear timeline. Memories don't always come in order, and that's okay. Let your mind wander naturally, from one period to another, without forcing chronology.

Capture both the small, seemingly mundane moments and the major milestones. Maybe you remember the first time you rode a bike or the excitement of your first day of school. Perhaps you recall the laughter shared with friends during summer vacations or the smell of home-cooked meals. These ordinary moments are vital - they form the foundation of your daily life, even if they don't feel significant compared to trauma. They matter, too.

At the same time, allow your mind to bring up the difficult experiences: your first encounter with loss, moments of rejection, heartbreaks, and, of course, the traumas that have left deeper scars. Write them all down without filtering or minimizing any part of your journey.

This process is meant to be comprehensive - you are not just documenting trauma, but your entire life, the highs, the lows, and everything in between.

4. Continue Writing Until You Reach the Present

Let your memory guide you through the different stages of your life - childhood, adolescence, early adulthood, and beyond. There's no need to rush. The goal is not to capture every detail but to explore the range of your experiences, both big and small, happy and sad.

You might find that certain periods are easier to remember than others. Some memories might come flooding back with vivid detail, while others feel distant or fragmented. This is natural. Memories are not linear or static - they ebb and flow, and certain periods may stand out more than others.

When you encounter gaps or feel stuck, don't force yourself to fill in the blanks. Simply move forward to the next memory that feels accessible. The process should feel fluid, allowing your mind to drift through the various chapters of your life at its own pace.

5. Stop When You Feel You've Exhausted Your Memories

At some point, you will likely feel that you've captured all the significant memories you can recall. This may leave you with a collection of fragmented snapshots, some clear, some hazy - but that's perfectly fine. The goal of this exercise is not to create a detailed account of your entire life but to observe the selectivity of memory - to see what stands out and what fades into the background.

By this stage, you should have a written collection of moments that define your life's journey. These memories, both major and minor, offer a window into the full range of your experiences, not just the moments of trauma.

Reflect on What You've Written

Now that you've completed the exercise, take time to reflect on what you've written. Look for patterns. What stands out to you? What moments are clearest in your mind? Were there any periods of your life that were particularly difficult to recall? How much of your memory is dominated by trauma or pain? How much is centered around neutral or positive experiences?

As you review your memories, you may begin to notice that trauma, while intense, only represents a fraction of your total lived experience. There are likely many moments - small, seemingly ordinary events - that were overshadowed by the emotional weight of trauma. These everyday experiences, though they may seem insignificant, are just as much a part of your life as the difficult times.

This reflection helps you see that your life is not just defined by the most painful moments - it is a tapestry woven with countless other threads, each one adding depth and meaning to the whole.

Calculate the Percentage of Life Tied to Trauma

This step is essential for gaining perspective on the role trauma plays in your life. Consider your age - perhaps you are 30, 40, or 50. Let's use an example: if you are 40 years old, you've lived approximately 14,600 days. Now, reflect on how much time has been consumed by trauma. Even if your traumatic experiences lasted for a few years, say three or four, that still leaves over 10,000 days of your life that were not defined by trauma.

When you look at the numbers, it becomes clear: while trauma feels monumental, it is only one chapter in the book of your life. This realization can be incredibly freeing. You begin to see that trauma, while important, is not the entirety of your story. You are more than your suffering.

The Reframing Component: Shifting the Narrative

One of the most powerful aspects of the healing process is reframing the narrative - taking a closer look at your life and consciously reshaping the way you understand and tell your own story. This isn't just about chronicling the events of your life; it's about altering the lens through which you view your experiences, especially the painful ones. Reframing allows you to challenge the long-held beliefs that trauma is the defining feature of your existence. Instead, you begin to see trauma as just one part of a larger, more complex story - one where joy, resilience, and growth also play a significant role.

In this section, we'll dive into the reasons why this exercise is so impactful and how you can use it to reshape your narrative, giving you greater emotional freedom and a more balanced perspective on your life.

Selective Memory and Emotional Weight

One of the reasons trauma feels so all-encompassing is because of how our brains process emotional experiences. Humans are wired to prioritize negative and traumatic memories because they're tied to survival. Emotionally intense events activate the amygdala, the brain's center for fear and threat detection, which ensures that these memories are deeply imprinted in our minds. This survival mechanism is useful in dangerous situations, but when it comes to trauma, it can distort our perception of our lives.

Over time, this leads to a phenomenon known as selective memory, where negative or traumatic events take up far more space in our emotional memory than neutral or positive experiences. Your brain, constantly scanning for danger, keeps bringing the traumatic memory to the forefront, while the everyday moments - the peaceful mornings, the laughter with friends, the quiet moments of contentment - fade into the background.

This selective memory distorts your understanding of your life. Trauma becomes magnified, casting a long shadow over your past and making it seem as though those painful events define who you are. By reframing your narrative, you challenge this cognitive distortion, forcing your brain to recognize the richness and fullness of your life beyond the trauma.

Life's Fullness and Complexity

Mapping out the entirety of your life isn't about erasing trauma; it's about recognizing the complexity of your story. Every life is a tapestry woven from countless threads - some dark, some light, but all essential to its full picture. When you look at your life holistically, you begin to realize that while trauma may be a part of your story, it's not the only part.

Your life contains a wealth of experiences, many of which have been neutral or even joyful, but these have been overshadowed by the emotional weight of trauma. By engaging in this exercise, you start to appreciate how these experiences coexist alongside the painful ones. The quiet mornings sipping coffee, the warm hug of a loved one, the personal victories and small moments of joy - all of these threads are vital parts of the tapestry that is your life.

As you lay out your experiences, you'll start to see patterns that help you understand your personal evolution. You'll notice that even in times of struggle, you've found moments of peace, and that in times of chaos, you've still experienced love and connection. This recognition of life's complexity allows you to shift your perspective, from seeing your life as a series of hardships to recognizing the full spectrum of human experience.

Reshaping Your Story

One of the most transformative aspects of reframing your narrative is the opportunity it gives you to reshape the story you tell yourself. For many people who have experienced trauma, the dominant narrative becomes one of victimhood or survival, with trauma serving as the central theme. While trauma is a part of your story, it doesn't have to be the defining chapter. Through this exercise, you can actively work to rewrite your relationship with the past.

Think about the language you use when you describe your life. Do you focus solely on the hardships? Do you downplay your moments of joy, strength, or success? This exercise allows you to consciously change the way you speak about your past, present, and future. Instead of framing yourself solely as a survivor of trauma, you can begin to see yourself as someone who has grown through the experience, someone who has not only endured suffering but who has also found meaning, connection, and purpose along the way.

For Sarah, the process of reshaping her story was profound. After her traumatic accident, she initially saw herself through the lens of her suffering - an injured person, emotionally and physically. The accident dominated her perception of herself and her life. However, as Sarah began to map out the entirety of her life, she started to see that the accident, while significant, was just one chapter. It didn't erase the deep connections she had with her children, the joy she had found in her career before the trauma, or the resilience she had demonstrated in overcoming previous hardships.

By reframing her narrative, Sarah was able to shift from seeing herself as broken to recognizing her strength, adaptability, and capacity for growth. This shift didn't happen overnight, but with each reflection on her life's fullness, she saw herself less as a victim of fate and more as an active author of her own story.

The Power of Reframing

Reframing your narrative is a deeply empowering process. It reminds you that while trauma may have changed you, it does not define you. You are more than the sum of your painful experiences. You are the sum of all your experiences - the good, the bad, the joyful, and the heartbreaking.

This exercise isn't about denying the importance of your trauma or pretending that it wasn't life-altering. Instead, it's about balancing the narrative, so that your story reflects the full reality of your life, rather than just the most painful parts. Trauma may be part of the picture, but it's not the whole picture.

When you engage in this practice of reframing, you give yourself the gift of perspective. You see your life not as a series of disconnected, chaotic events, but as a journey of growth and discovery. This shift in narrative doesn't diminish the significance of your trauma, but it puts it in context, allowing you to move forward with a greater sense of clarity and purpose.

Rewriting the Next Chapter

Finally, perhaps the most powerful aspect of reframing your narrative is that it allows you to become the author of your future. By reshaping your relationship with the past, you gain the freedom to decide how the next chapters of your life will unfold. Trauma no longer holds the pen; you do.

You can start to envision a future where you're not defined by what happened to you but by how you choose to move forward. This doesn't mean that the trauma is forgotten or that healing is complete. Rather, it means that you are no longer beholden to the narrative of victimhood. You can write your own story of resilience, of new beginnings, of self-discovery.

As you reframe your narrative, you begin to see that your life is not a single story of pain, but a complex, beautiful, and evolving journey. Each moment - whether joyful, painful, or mundane - has contributed to the person you are today. And as you look ahead, you have the power to write the story of the person you will become.

Reclaiming Your Story

Reframing your narrative is one of the most profound steps you can take toward healing. It shifts the way you see yourself, your past, and your future. By challenging the cognitive distortions that trauma creates, you gain the ability to see your life in its entirety, acknowledging both the hardships and the moments of joy and growth. You are no longer defined by your trauma, but by the full, rich complexity of your experiences.

Through this exercise, you take back control of your story. You become the author, writing not just about what has happened to you, but about how you have grown through it and who you are becoming. You reclaim your narrative and, in doing so, reclaim your life.

Did this exercise help me realize that trauma, while significant, does not define my entire life?

The purpose of this exercise is not to minimize trauma, but to reposition it. Trauma is undoubtedly impactful, often deeply so, but it is not the defining feature of your entire existence. Ask yourself: What else defines me? As you review the memories you've written down, reflect on the range of experiences that shaped you - your relationships, your accomplishments, your passions, your ordinary moments of contentment.

This exercise helps to redistribute emotional weight. Trauma may have occupied a central place in your identity for a long time, but now you have the opportunity to view it from a new angle. You can begin to see that your life includes far more than those painful moments. Trauma is part of your journey, but it is not your entire story.

Take a moment to breathe deeply and sit with this realization. Trauma, while painful and difficult, does not have to dominate your sense of self. You are not just the sum of your suffering. You are a person shaped by countless experiences, relationships, and moments of growth that have contributed to the richness and depth of your life.

What positive or neutral memories surfaced during this exercise that I had forgotten?

One of the most profound revelations that can come from this exercise is the rediscovery of forgotten or overlooked moments. Often, in the shadow of trauma, the small, everyday joys or even neutral experiences fade into the background. Yet these moments - no matter how seemingly insignificant - are crucial because they reflect the normalcy and stability that trauma may have temporarily obscured.

As you review your life map, consider the positive memories that surfaced. What did you recall that you had forgotten? Perhaps you remembered childhood adventures, shared laughter with loved ones, or quiet moments of peace. These experiences are just as real and valid as your traumatic memories, yet they may have been neglected because they don't carry the same emotional intensity.

Even neutral memories - the rhythm of daily life, routines, or casual conversations - are valuable. They remind you that much of life exists in a steady flow of moments that are neither extraordinary nor painful, but simply are. These neutral or positive moments make up the vast majority of our lived experience.

Reflect on what this says about your life as a whole. How can you honor these rediscovered memories? How can you allow them to take up more space in your emotional and mental landscape? By giving these moments the attention they deserve, you begin to shift the balance in your life story, allowing joy, peace, and neutrality to take a more central role.

How can I begin to shift my focus away from letting trauma dominate my identity and instead see it as one part of a larger life story?

Now that you've gained a broader perspective on your life, the next step is to actively work on reshaping your personal narrative. Trauma, while significant, doesn't have to be the central story you tell yourself or others. It can be a chapter in your life, not the whole book.

Shifting your focus is about consciously choosing to prioritize other aspects of your life - your resilience, your strengths, your moments of joy, and even your moments of quiet neutrality. Here are some strategies for doing this:

Daily Affirmations of Wholeness: Each day, remind yourself that you are more than your trauma. Write or say affirmations that reinforce your identity beyond pain. For example, "I am resilient, strong, and more than the hardships I've faced," or "My life is rich with experiences, both joyful and painful, and I choose to honor them all."

Cultivate Gratitude for Neutral Moments: Often, we overlook the small, everyday moments of peace because they don't demand our attention in the same way that trauma does. But these neutral moments are vital - they provide the foundation for a stable and balanced life. Each day, make a habit of acknowledging and appreciating the ordinary - whether it's your morning coffee, a walk in the park, or a quiet moment before bed.

Rewrite Your Story: Take some time to rewrite the story of your life, focusing on the whole picture. Include the traumas, but also highlight the moments of growth, love, resilience, and joy. Write about the lessons you've learned, the people who have supported you, and the ways in which you've transformed. This act of rewriting can be incredibly empowering - it puts you in control of your narrative.

Shift Your Self-Perception: Often, trauma leads us to believe that we are broken, incomplete, or damaged. Challenge this self-perception by reflecting on your strengths. What have you overcome? What skills, abilities, and qualities have you developed through your experiences? Recognize that your survival is a testament to your strength.

Create a Life Map of the Future: Now that you've mapped out your past, consider mapping out the future. What do you want your life to look like moving forward? Where do you want to direct your energy? This can be a powerful way to shift your focus from dwelling on trauma to actively shaping the life you want to live.

Moving Toward a Balanced, Empowered Narrative

By recognizing that trauma is only a fraction of your total life experience, you begin to gain the perspective necessary for healing. You see that while trauma has shaped you, it does not have the power to define you. There are thousands of moments, neutral or positive, that have also played a role in who you are. By acknowledging this, you can start to shift your narrative toward one that is more balanced, hopeful, and empowered.

This new understanding is liberating. It allows you to break free from the confines of a trauma-focused identity and embrace the full complexity of your life. You are not just a survivor of trauma; you are also a person who has experienced joy, connection, growth, and countless ordinary moments of peace. And it is through this holistic view of your life that true healing begins.

Your trauma, while real and painful, is not the entirety of who you are. By embracing the fullness of your lived experience, you reclaim your narrative and step forward with clarity, strength, and purpose.

Sarah's Journey to Finding Meaning

As we return to Sarah's story, we witness her progress from the initial phases of grounding, emotional detachment, and time-based reframing, through the practice of Select What Matters. She has learned to focus her emotional energy on what truly matters and to let go of the burdens that do not serve her. Now, in this final stage, Sarah must confront the deeper question: What does my trauma mean in the larger context of my life?

Initially, Sarah's car accident seemed like an unmitigated disaster - something that tore apart the fabric of her life and left her feeling powerless. She lost her sense of security, her confidence, and, at times, her hope. But as Sarah progressed through the previous steps of the

R.E.S.T. framework, she began to distance herself emotionally from the raw intensity of the trauma. She learned how to regulate her emotional responses, to let go of unnecessary pressures, and to focus on what mattered most. Now, she must integrate this traumatic event into a broader narrative, discovering what it can teach her and how it can help her grow.

Reframing Suffering Through Meaning

The final stage of Sarah's journey involves finding meaning in the accident, not by diminishing its significance or pretending it wasn't painful, but by reframing it within the context of her evolving life story.

Instead of seeing the accident as a moment of devastation, Sarah begins to ask herself new questions:

What has this experience taught me about myself?

How has this changed the way I value my time, relationships, and personal boundaries?

What strengths have I discovered within myself as I've navigated this journey of recovery?

As Sarah reflects on these questions, she realizes that the accident, though deeply traumatic, opened her eyes to aspects of

her life she had previously overlooked. Before the accident, Sarah had been operating on autopilot - pushing herself to meet external expectations, overextending herself for others, and neglecting her own needs in the process. The accident forced her to slow down, to confront the fragility of life, and to reassess what truly mattered to her.

By applying the principles of Logotherapy, Sarah begins to see that her trauma, while painful, offered her an opportunity for transformation. The accident became a catalyst for change - a moment that pushed her to realign her life with her core values. This shift in perspective is central to the Transform Meaning phase of the R.E.S.T. framework. It's about understanding that suffering, while inevitable, can be reframed as a source of growth, meaning, and purpose.

The Power of Meaning-Making

Finding meaning in suffering does not happen overnight, nor does it negate the pain of the experience itself. Instead, it allows you to contextualize your suffering within the larger narrative of your life. For Sarah, this meant acknowledging that the accident wasn't just an event that derailed her life - it was also an opportunity to re-evaluate her priorities and make changes that aligned with her deeper sense of purpose.

One of the most profound shifts Sarah experiences is a newfound sense of resilience. She begins to understand that surviving the accident wasn't just about physical healing - it was about emotional and spiritual growth. The accident revealed her inner strength, her ability to adapt, and her capacity for self-compassion. Through her journey of recovery, Sarah found that she could handle far more than she once thought possible, and that realization became a cornerstone of her new sense of self.

Real-World Application: Embracing Transform Meaning in Your Life

As we journey through life, we inevitably encounter moments of deep pain and suffering. Trauma, whether from personal loss, adversity, or unexpected change, can make the world seem meaningless, unfair, or devoid of hope. Yet, through the principles of Logotherapy and the search for Transform Meaning, we can begin to reframe our experiences - not to erase the suffering but to transform it into something that contributes to our growth, resilience, and purpose.

In this section, we will explore how you can apply these principles to your own life, just as Sarah did. By taking concrete steps to acknowledge your pain, reframe your thinking, and find meaning in your suffering, you can begin to rebuild your inner world with a deeper sense of purpose and empowerment. Let's dive into the practical ways you can embark on this transformative journey.

1. Acknowledge the Pain

The first step toward healing and finding meaning in trauma is to acknowledge the pain. So often, we feel the need to downplay or suppress our suffering, whether out of fear, guilt, or the belief that we need to be "strong" for others. However, this only serves to prolong the healing process. Healing requires honesty, both with yourself and others.

In acknowledging your pain, you give yourself permission to feel it fully. This is not about wallowing in despair, but about honoring the depth of your experience. It's important to recognize that your trauma is real, and your feelings - whether they are of sadness, anger, confusion, or even numbness - are valid. These emotions are part of the natural human response to suffering. Denying them only keeps you stuck.

For Sarah, acknowledging her pain meant admitting that she wasn't as okay as she pretended to be after her accident. She had tried to hold everything together - at work, at home, and in her relationships - believing that showing vulnerability would make her appear weak. But it wasn't until she allowed herself to feel the grief, fear, and frustration of her situation that she began to open the door to healing. She realized that her suffering didn't need to be hidden, nor did it diminish her strength.

By acknowledging your pain, you take the first crucial step toward healing. You stop running from the trauma and instead face it with courage, accepting that it is part of your journey.

2. Shift the Focus

Once you've acknowledged your pain, the next step is to shift your focus from the question of "Why did this happen to me?" to "What can I learn from this?" This shift in focus is central to the principles of Logotherapy, which teaches that while we cannot always change the circumstances of our suffering, we can always change how we interpret them.

It's natural to ask "Why me?" when we are in the midst of trauma. This question, while understandable, keeps us locked in a cycle of victimhood, where the focus remains on the unfairness of the situation rather than on what we can do to grow beyond it. Logotherapy challenges us to move beyond this mindset and ask more empowering questions: What can I take away from this experience? How can this suffering contribute to my evolution?

For Sarah, shifting the focus meant reframing her trauma not as a senseless accident, but as a turning point in her life. Initially, she had fixated on the injustice of her suffering - she was a careful driver, a loving mother, someone who didn't deserve this kind of pain. But as she began to practice the principles of Transform Meaning, she asked herself different questions: What can I learn from this experience? How has this trauma reshaped my priorities and values? By doing so, she stopped focusing on the randomness of the accident and instead began to see how it could help her redefine her life.

This shift in focus doesn't mean the trauma suddenly becomes positive or that the suffering disappears. Rather, it allows you to engage with the trauma in a way that fosters personal growth. It's the act of turning your gaze away from what was lost and toward what can still be gained.

3. Seek Strengths

Amidst the pain of trauma, it can be difficult to see anything other than the immediate loss, grief, or fear. Yet, even in the darkest of times, we often discover strengths we didn't know we had. Trauma can reveal resilience, courage, resourcefulness, and other inner qualities that emerge as we navigate our way through adversity.

To begin finding meaning in your suffering, it's essential to reflect on the strengths you've uncovered along the way. Ask yourself: What have I learned about myself through this experience? What qualities have I displayed that have helped me survive?

In Sarah's case, she found that the accident, while traumatic, had awakened a deeper sense of resilience in her. She had always thought of herself as a person who needed control, but through the trauma, she discovered that she could handle chaos and uncertainty far better than she ever imagined. Her ability to care for her children, even in the midst of her own pain, showed her a level of strength she hadn't known she possessed.

When we focus on our strengths, we shift from seeing ourselves as victims of circumstance to recognizing the power within us. This recognition is a vital step in finding meaning in trauma because it allows us to see the ways in which suffering can deepen our understanding of ourselves. We become more aware of our capabilities, our resilience, and our capacity to endure.

4. Find Purpose in the Pain

Finding meaning in suffering is not a one-size-fits-all process. It takes time, reflection, and, most importantly, patience with yourself. One of the most profound ways to create meaning from trauma is by discovering how your experience can serve a larger purpose - whether for yourself, for others, or for the world.

Finding purpose doesn't necessarily mean transforming your trauma into a public cause or lifelong mission. It can be as simple as recognizing how the experience has shaped your perspective on life, deepened your empathy for others, or clarified what truly matters to you. Sometimes, the meaning we find in suffering comes through helping others who are going through something similar or by sharing our stories in ways that inspire or comfort.

For Sarah, finding purpose in her pain meant becoming more attuned to the present moment and prioritizing her relationships. Before the accident, she had been so focused on career success and external validation that she often overlooked the importance of simply being with her children, her friends, and herself. The trauma forced her to reevaluate her priorities, and she realized that what mattered most was not how much she achieved, but how deeply she connected with the people she loved.

As you reflect on your own trauma, consider how the experience might serve as a turning point in your life. Ask yourself: How has this experience changed me? What new values or perspectives have emerged? How can I use this pain to bring more meaning to my life?

Perhaps your suffering has made you more compassionate, more patient, or more aware of the preciousness of life. Maybe it has given you the motivation to pursue a different path, one that aligns more closely with your true self. Whatever the case, finding purpose in your pain allows you to transform suffering into something constructive - a force for growth and change.

5. Integrate the Experience

The final and perhaps most important step in finding meaning through trauma is integration. Integration means accepting that your trauma is a part of your life, but it does not define who you are. It becomes one chapter in the larger narrative of your life - one that has shaped you, but not one that limits you.

Integration is about weaving the lessons of your suffering into the fabric of your personal growth. This doesn't mean the trauma disappears or that the pain is no longer there. It means that you carry the trauma with you in a way that is empowering, rather than debilitating. You allow the experience to teach you, to guide you, and to remind you of the strength and wisdom you've gained.

For Sarah, integration meant embracing the accident as a pivotal moment in her life, but not as the defining one. She learned to view the trauma as a source of resilience, compassion, and self-awareness, and she carried those lessons forward as she rebuilt her life. The accident would always be a part of her story, but it no longer controlled her narrative.

To integrate your own trauma, begin by reflecting on how the experience fits into the broader arc of your life. Ask yourself: How has this trauma influenced who I am today? What lessons have I learned, and how can I carry them forward? By integrating the experience, you allow the trauma to become a source of empowerment, rather than a source of despair.

Sarah's Transformation: A New Narrative

As Sarah continues to apply these principles, she begins to see herself in a new light. The accident is no longer the defining moment of her life, but a chapter in her larger journey of growth. She no longer views herself as someone who was broken by the accident; instead, she sees herself as someone who was transformed by it. The experience gave her the strength to prioritize her well-being, the courage to set boundaries, and the wisdom to focus on what truly mattered.

Sarah also found new ways to channel her experience into helping others. By sharing her story with friends and support groups, she was able to provide comfort to others going through similar hardships. In doing so, she discovered that her trauma could serve a purpose beyond her own healing - it could help others find strength and meaning in their own suffering.

The Role of Transform Meaning in Healing

The final phase of the R.E.S.T. framework - Transform Meaning - is about finding a sense of purpose and direction in the aftermath of trauma. It's the culmination of the previous steps, where grounding, emotional detachment, time-based reframing, and select what matters come together to help you reframe your suffering as part of your personal growth.

For Sarah, this journey led to profound insights about herself and the world around her. She learned that suffering, while painful, could be transformed into something meaningful. By embracing this final stage, she was able to integrate her trauma into her life in a way that allowed her to move forward with a sense of peace, resilience, and purpose.

In the same way, you can begin to find meaning in your own suffering. It may not be easy, and it may not happen right away, but by shifting your perspective and looking for the lessons within the pain, you can transform your trauma into a source of strength and wisdom. The key to this transformation is understanding that while suffering is an inevitable part of life, how we respond to it - and the meaning we attach to it - can define our path to healing and personal growth.

As we close Sarah's story, we invite you to embark on your own journey of finding meaning in adversity, using the tools of the R.E.S.T. framework to guide you toward a life of resilience, empowerment, and deeper purpose.

R.E.S.T. Practice

Applying Transform Meaning: Building a Life Beyond What Happened

This chapter helps you build meaning without glorifying trauma, excusing harm, or pretending pain was necessary.

Release: What needs to settle before you analyze this?

____

____

____

____

Examine Through Time: How might this feel or look different with time, distance, and support?

____

____

____

____

Select What Matters: What truly deserves your energy here?

____

____

____

____

Transform Meaning: What meaning can be built without minimizing what happened?

____

____

____

____

Reflection Prompts

- What meaning can I build without pretending the trauma was acceptable?

____

____

- What has survival taught me about what I value?

____

____

- What kind of life do I want to build from here?

____

____

Gentle Reminder

Do not force insight before your body has enough safety to hold it. Regulation comes before interpretation. You can return to any exercise slowly, briefly, and with support.

Daily Micro-Practice

Transform Meaning

Use this page as a brief daily practice. The point is repetition, not perfection. One honest sentence is enough.

Today I noticed:

____

____

____

____

The trauma-shaped story that appeared was:

____

____

____

____

The R.E.S.T. response I want to practice is:

____

____

____

____

One gentle action I can take next is:

____

____

____

____

Chapter 8

The R.E.S.T. Method in Practice

Long-Term Resilience

As you've worked through the stages of the R.E.S.T. model - Release, Integrate, Select What Matters, and Transform Meaning - you've likely felt profound shifts in the way you relate to your trauma and view yourself. This model does not offer a quick fix but instead guides you through an ongoing process of deep inner transformation, gradually removing layers of pain, distorted beliefs, and emotional chaos that trauma often brings.

In this chapter, we focus on how to build long-term resilience using the R.E.S.T. model as a tool that continues to serve you beyond the immediate work of trauma processing. The model functions like a funnel, starting with wide, tangled emotions and experiences, and narrowing down as you move through each stage. Ultimately, what's left is the core - the deepest truths that will help you understand your trauma and derive Transform Meaning from it.

Resilience is not about eliminating pain or avoiding difficulty. It's about your ability to adapt, recover, and grow stronger in the face of adversity. While trauma fundamentally changes us, it doesn't have to diminish us. Instead, when survivors learn to process their experiences and focus on what truly matters, they cultivate a resilience that empowers them, leading not only to healing but to thriving.

The Process of Unraveling

Healing from trauma is rarely straightforward; it's not a linear process but a journey with many twists and turns. You've likely encountered moments of clarity followed by periods of confusion, stretches of peace punctuated by waves of emotional struggle. The idea that healing is a simple endpoint is misleading. Instead, it's an ongoing process of unraveling the noise, identifying what is essential, and letting go of what isn't.

The R.E.S.T. model helps guide this process, acting as a funnel through which you sift your trauma, sorting through the emotional noise and cognitive distortions to distill your experience down to the most meaningful elements. Imagine trauma as a knot - twisted and intertwined thoughts, feelings, and beliefs. Each stage of R.E.S.T. helps you pull apart these threads, eventually leaving you with clarity, purpose, and peace.

Release: The First Step Toward Emotional Clarity

The first phase of R.E.S.T. is Release, where you begin by letting go of the immediate emotional charge associated with your trauma. Traumatic experiences often leave us overwhelmed with raw emotions, keeping us stuck in a cycle of intense distress. Release is not about ignoring your feelings or pushing them aside; it's about learning to observe them without being consumed by them.

Grounding techniques, mindfulness, and deep breathing exercises are key tools here, helping you detach from the overwhelming emotional intensity. By practicing Release, you start to clear away the emotional fog that trauma often creates, creating space to engage with your experience more thoughtfully and deliberately.

This phase is akin to removing the first layer of debris in the funnel - clearing out the reactive emotions and beginning to observe trauma from a calmer, more centered place.

Integrate: Weaving Trauma Into Your Life Narrative

Once you've achieved some emotional clarity, the next step is to Integrate your trauma into the broader story of your life. Trauma tends to dominate our internal narrative, making it difficult to see anything beyond the pain. Integration means placing the trauma in context - not minimizing it, but ensuring it becomes one part of your story, not the whole.

Cognitive reframing is a powerful tool in this phase. By challenging distorted thoughts - whether they are feelings of guilt, shame, or unworthiness - you begin to replace negative patterns with more balanced perspectives. This doesn't erase the trauma but helps you understand that it fits within the entire scope of your life. Alongside the trauma are moments of joy, growth, and strength.

As you work through Integrate, the funnel narrows. You've cleared away some of the emotional reactivity, and now you are starting to unravel the mental distortions left in the trauma's wake. Each distorted belief that falls away brings you closer to the core issues - the lessons your trauma holds and how they fit into your broader existence.

Select What Matters: Choosing What Matters

The third stage, Select What Matters, marks a significant turning point in your healing journey. After releasing the emotional charge of trauma and beginning to integrate it into your life narrative, Select What Matters challenges you to critically examine where you have been placing your emotional and mental energy. Trauma can leave us in a state of hypervigilance, feeling responsible for every emotion, every task, and every interaction. This stage allows you to step back and assess whether everything you've been carrying is truly yours to bear.

Select What Matters is about freedom from unnecessary burdens. It gives you permission to say, "This does not matter." It's a profound realization that not everything deserves your emotional investment. When you've been in survival mode for so long, as trauma often forces you to be, it can feel like everything is a threat or everything requires your attention. Select What Matters helps you shed that mindset by showing you that most things - especially the expectations imposed by society or even the unrealistic expectations you impose on yourself - do not matter nearly as much as you think they do.

For example, Sarah, our protagonist, had been emotionally investing in areas that were depleting her. At work, she strived for perfection to prove that her accident hadn't affected her capabilities. Socially, she overextended herself, always trying to be everything to everyone. In this phase, Sarah learned to apply Select What Matters, choosing where her emotional energy would be most valuable. By letting go of the need to be perfect at work or the perfect friend and mother, she freed herself from emotional exhaustion.

Select What Matters, therefore, becomes a powerful filtration system in your healing process. You shed the layers of unnecessary emotional investment, creating a clearer path to what truly matters. As the funnel narrows, so too do your priorities, leaving you with only the core issues that demand your attention.

Transform Meaning: The Core of Healing

At the heart of the R.E.S.T. model, after peeling away the unnecessary emotional weight and mental distortions, lies the final and most transformative stage: Transform Meaning.

Transform Meaning is where trauma survivors find their most profound healing. In this stage, after you've released emotional reactivity, integrated trauma into your larger life narrative, and selectively let go of what doesn't matter, you are left with the task of making meaning out of your suffering. This is the culmination of the R.E.S.T. model - it's not enough to simply heal the wounds of trauma; the ultimate goal is to grow from the experience, to use it as a platform for a deeper understanding of yourself, others, and life itself.

Transform Meaning invites you to ask the most fundamental questions:

What has this trauma taught me about who I am?

How can I use this experience to enrich my life, rather than diminish it?

What deeper understanding of life, relationships, or resilience has this experience brought me?

This is not about minimizing trauma. It's about finding purpose in your pain. When you can derive meaning from your suffering, it transforms from a force that holds you back to one that propels you forward. It becomes part of your growth, not just a scar on your past.

For Sarah, finding meaning transformation wasn't an immediate realization. It came through the gradual process of working through her trauma using the R.E.S.T. model. In the end, she found that her trauma had deepened her sense of empathy and allowed her to reframe her relationship with her family and children in profound ways. Instead of seeing herself solely as a victim of her accident, she now saw herself as a person who had emerged with a stronger sense of purpose - to live more fully, be more present, and to help others through their own traumatic experiences.

Daily R.E.S.T. Practice: Sustaining Your Healing

Healing is not a destination you arrive at one day, perfectly whole and untouched by your past. Instead, it's an ongoing journey - a practice. Like anything worth mastering, healing takes time, repetition, and patience. Some days you may feel strong and steady, full of purpose and clarity. Other days, the old wounds may open again, or new challenges may emerge, pulling you back into the very places you thought you had left behind. This is why the practice of healing must be daily. It's not something you check off a list and forget about. It's a way of life.

The R.E.S.T. model - Release, Examine Through Time, Select What Matters, and Transform Meaning - guides you in building resilience, not just by addressing the trauma of the past, but by equipping you to face the emotional turbulence of everyday life. This model offers you a framework, a structure to lean on when life feels chaotic or overwhelming. It's a way to navigate not only what has hurt you but also what continues to challenge you. When you make R.E.S.T. a daily practice, you are committing to yourself and your emotional well-being in a profound and powerful way.

This isn't a practice about perfection. There will be days when it feels natural and easy, and others where each step feels like walking through quicksand. The key is consistency - showing up for yourself every day, no matter how hard or how easy it may feel. Through this consistency, you cultivate not only healing but resilience - the kind that endures. With each day, you reinforce your commitment to yourself and your growth, allowing you to move forward even when the past tries to pull you back.

A Roadmap to Emotional Clarity: The Daily R.E.S.T. Practice

The Daily R.E.S.T. Practice is not just a method for processing trauma; it's a daily commitment to fostering your emotional well-being and personal growth. It's a roadmap for navigating life's complexities with resilience, clarity, and purpose. Each step in the R.E.S.T. model acts as a compass, guiding you through the highs and lows of life, helping you let go of what no longer serves you, broaden your perspective, focus on what truly matters, and find deeper meaning even in the most difficult moments.

This practice is a way of approaching your emotional world with intention, providing structure for reflection and transformation. Let's dive deeper into each of these steps to see how they work together to create long-term resilience.

1. Release (5–10 minutes)

Release is the first step of the R.E.S.T. practice - a deliberate act of letting go of the emotional weight you've accumulated throughout the day. Without realizing it, we carry emotional baggage from moment to moment: a conversation that went wrong, a stressful work deadline, or an unresolved personal issue. These burdens stack up, making us feel heavy and emotionally cluttered. If not addressed, they can make it difficult to stay present or think clearly.

The purpose of Release is to give yourself permission to unburden these emotions, even temporarily, so that you can move forward more freely. It's like setting down a heavy backpack that you've carried for too long.

Imagine this scenario: Sarah had a rough day at work. A tense meeting with her boss left her feeling frustrated, and her to-do list only seemed to grow longer as the day progressed. By the time she gets home, she's not only physically tired but mentally overloaded. Instead of diving headfirst into her evening responsibilities, Sarah pauses. She takes a few moments to sit in silence, breathing deeply. With each exhale, she visualizes releasing the stress that's been sitting on her chest. After just a few minutes, she feels lighter, as if the tension has melted away, giving her a clearer, calmer mind to engage with her evening.

Practice:

Grounding Exercise: Use the 5-4-3-2-1 method to bring yourself back into the present moment. Start by identifying five things you can see, four things you can touch, three things you can hear, two things you can smell, and one thing you can taste. This exercise helps you pull yourself out of emotional overwhelm and ground yourself in the now.

Deep Breathing: With each inhale, visualize drawing in a sense of peace. With each exhale, release the tightness, worry, or stress you've been holding onto. Let each breath clear the emotional clutter from the day.

Purpose:

The purpose of Release is to create emotional space, a clean slate, so you can face the present moment with clarity. Life's demands often cloud our ability to be present. By consciously letting go of the emotional burdens that have piled up, you allow yourself to step into the next moment feeling lighter and more centered.

2. Examine Through Time(10–15 minutes)

When we're in the thick of emotional pain, it feels as if the moment we're in is all that exists. Time seems to collapse around us, and we can't imagine a future where the pain eases. Time-Based Reframing helps you step back and view your current challenges through the lens of time. It reminds you that healing is a gradual process and that the emotional intensity you're experiencing now will eventually soften.

Let's look at Tom: After a painful breakup, Tom feels consumed by heartbreak. It's as if his entire world has been turned upside down, and he can't see beyond the immediate grief. In his daily R.E.S.T. practice, Tom uses Time-Based Reframing to imagine his life six months from now. He pictures himself reconnecting with friends, rediscovering his passions, and finding moments of peace. He's not expecting an instant fix, but this visualization gives him hope. It shows him that while the pain is very real, it is also temporary.

By practicing this step, Tom gains perspective. He can see that his life is still unfolding, and today's pain will eventually be woven into a larger narrative that includes healing, growth, and new beginnings.

Practice:

Visualization: Close your eyes and imagine your future self - whether it's six months, a year, or even five years from now. Picture yourself looking back on this moment. How do you feel about the struggles you're facing now? What wisdom or strength have you gained? This practice reminds you that time itself is a healer.

Reflection: Think back to a difficult experience from your past that once seemed insurmountable. Reflect on how time has changed your perspective on that event. What seemed all-consuming at the time may now feel distant or even instructive. This reflection reminds you that today's pain will also fade.

Time-Based Reframing provides the gift of perspective. It's a way of reminding yourself that pain is part of the moment, but it's not permanent. By looking ahead to a time when today's struggles feel more manageable, you cultivate patience, hope, and a deeper trust in the process of healing.

3. Select What Matters (5 minutes)

In today's fast-paced world, we often feel overwhelmed by all the demands on our time and energy. We're taught that everything matters - that every email must be answered, every task must be done perfectly, and every relationship must be managed. But the truth is, not everything deserves your attention. Select What Matters is about reclaiming your emotional freedom by recognizing that some things simply don't matter in the grand scheme of life. It's the art of letting go of what isn't essential.

Consider Rebecca, a mother and corporate executive who constantly feels like she's juggling too many balls. She spends her day worrying about her children's academic progress, the success of her team at work, and the perception others have of her. One night, she engages in her R.E.S.T. practice and asks herself, "What truly matters today?" She realizes she's been investing a lot of emotional energy in areas that don't align with her core values, such as her need to be seen as perfect at work. That night, Rebecca lets go of the pressure to excel in every area and instead focuses on being present with her children. Through Select What Matters, she frees herself from unnecessary emotional burdens and refocuses on what's truly important.

Practice:

Emotional Audit: Take a few moments to review your day and ask yourself: "Where did I spend my emotional energy today? Did it align with my core values?" Identify areas where you invested too much energy in things that don't deserve it and give yourself permission to let go.

Releasing Control: Recognize that many things are outside your control - other people's opinions, the future, and even some outcomes you've been striving for. Select What Matters encourages you to release the need for control over these things, allowing you to reclaim your emotional energy for what truly matters.

Select What Matters is about prioritizing your energy and letting go of the things that drain you unnecessarily. It teaches you to focus on what aligns with your values and goals, rather than scattering your emotional resources on every little detail. By focusing your energy only on what truly matters, you create more space for peace and clarity in your life.

4. Transform Meaning (10–15 minutes)

At the heart of the human experience is the search for meaning. Trauma and adversity can shake our sense of purpose, leaving us feeling lost or disconnected from what matters most. The final step of the R.E.S.T. practice - Transform Meaning - is about taking the painful experiences you've endured and turning them into something purposeful. It's about defining yourself not by the trauma, but by how you choose to respond to it.

Maria, for example, lost her father unexpectedly, and for months, her grief seemed overwhelming. But as part of her R.E.S.T. practice, she began reflecting on what her grief had taught her. She realized that her father's death had deepened her empathy and motivated her to live more fully, carrying forward the values he had instilled in her. Maria then decided to volunteer at a hospice, helping others through their own losses. By finding Transform Meaning in her grief, she was able to transform her pain into a source of strength and connection.

Practice:

End-of-Day Reflection: Before you go to bed, spend a few moments reflecting on the day. What lessons did today offer you? How has this experience - no matter how difficult - helped you grow or better understand life? Even in the hardest moments, there is meaning to be found.

Gratitude Practice: Write down three things you're grateful for each night. This helps shift your focus from what is missing or painful to what is present and abundant in your life, allowing you to find meaning and connection even in tough times.

The purpose of Transform Meaning is to take the challenges life throws at you and use them as stepping stones for personal growth. It's not about erasing pain, but about integrating it into a larger story of purpose and resilience. This step reminds you that you have the power to turn suffering into strength, and it encourages you to live with greater intention and alignment with your deepest values.

The Daily R.E.S.T. Practice: A Path to Long-Term Resilience

The Daily R.E.S.T. Practice is more than a tool for healing trauma - it's a path to emotional clarity, resilience, and deeper meaning. Each step - Release, Examine Through Time, Select What Matters, and Transform Meaning - serves as a powerful reminder that you have the ability to navigate life's challenges with grace and strength. These steps work together to help you let go of unnecessary burdens, gain perspective on your struggles, focus your energy where it matters, and transform pain into purpose.

Your trauma is part of your story, but it doesn't define you. Through the R.E.S.T. model, you learn to transcend it - not by forgetting, but by integrating it into a larger narrative of growth and healing. Every day you engage with this practice, you are not only healing - you are evolving, building the resilience to face whatever life brings next.

You are not your trauma. You are your growth. And through the Daily R.E.S.T. Practice, you remind yourself of this truth, one step at a time.

The Power of Daily Practice: A Path to Resilience

The Daily R.E.S.T. Practice is not just a tool for processing trauma; it's a daily commitment to your emotional well-being and growth. Each step - Release, Examine Through Time, Select What Matters, and Transform Meaning - guides you through a process of letting go of unnecessary burdens, gaining perspective, prioritizing what matters, and finding deeper meaning in your experiences.

By returning to this practice every day, you strengthen your emotional muscles, enabling you to face life's inevitable challenges with greater resilience and grace. This practice reminds you that your trauma is part of your story, but it doesn't define you. Through the R.E.S.T. model, you learn to transcend your pain - not by erasing it, but by integrating it into the larger narrative of who you are becoming.

Every day that you engage with this practice, you are not just healing - you are evolving. You are becoming more resilient, more purposeful, and more capable of facing whatever comes next.

You are not your trauma. You are your growth. And with the Daily R.E.S.T. Practice, you remind yourself of this truth, one day at a time.

defined not by pain, but by resilience, meaning, and an unshakeable sense of purpose.

The R.E.S.T. Pathway: Refining Your Core Issues

The R.E.S.T. Pathway is more than a tool for healing - it is a process of refinement, a journey that helps you distill your trauma and emotions down to their essence. At its heart, this practice is about removing the excess, the emotional baggage and mental clutter, until all that remains are the truths you need to move forward. These truths form the core of your healing, guiding you through the darkest chapters of your story and helping you discover resilience and purpose on the other side.

Healing from trauma is often perceived as an additive process: more therapy, more techniques, more coping mechanisms. But in reality, healing is much more about letting go than adding on. The R.E.S.T. Pathway doesn't ask you to do more - it encourages you to do less, to shed what no longer serves you, and to simplify your emotional life. This process, over time, clarifies your path, leaving behind only the essentials, those pieces of wisdom and strength that carry you toward long-term resilience.

The Importance of Stripping Away the Layers

Trauma leaves behind layers - layers of emotional armor, cognitive distortions, and psychological defenses that once served to protect you. These layers may have helped you survive the initial impact of trauma, but over time, they become suffocating. They can trap you in cycles of self-blame, catastrophizing, and black-and-white thinking. And while these defense mechanisms might have been necessary in moments of intense pain, they become roadblocks to healing when left unchallenged.

Healing is about gradually dismantling these layers, and the R.E.S.T. Pathway serves as the tool that enables you to do this. Each step - Release, Examine Through Time, Select What Matters, and Transform Meaning - is like a filter, sifting through your emotions and beliefs, separating what's helpful from what's holding you back.

As you continue to move through the funnel, you begin to notice that certain thoughts, emotions, and beliefs - once so dominant - start to lose their grip on you. The weight of these distorted ideas begins to dissolve, and you start to see things more clearly. It's not that the pain vanishes, but rather, the intensity with which it once consumed you fades. You can begin to see your trauma for what it is - an experience that shaped you, but not one that defines you.

Healing, in this sense, is not an endpoint but a continuous process of stripping away the excess layers, one by one. With each layer that falls away, you come closer to the truth of who you are beneath the trauma, the essence of your strength, and the lessons that have been waiting to reveal themselves.

Creating Emotional Clarity: A Life Free of Fog

One of the most powerful outcomes of this funneling process is emotional clarity. Trauma has a way of muddying the waters of your emotional life. Feelings get tangled up in one another - guilt, anger, grief, fear - and it becomes difficult to understand where one ends and another begins. You might find yourself reacting to situations without fully understanding why, trapped in emotional loops that feel impossible to escape.

But as you move through the R.E.S.T. process, clarity begins to emerge. You start to identify the difference between a fleeting emotional reaction - like frustration over a minor inconvenience - and a deeper, more significant emotion tied to your trauma. This ability to distinguish between the two is life-changing. It allows you to stop being swept away by every emotional wave that comes your way. You become more grounded, more centered, able to respond to life's challenges rather than react impulsively.

Emotional clarity doesn't mean you stop feeling. On the contrary, it means you feel with greater accuracy. You're able to sit with your emotions, understand their origins, and decide what to do with them. You no longer feel like a victim of your feelings, but rather, a steward of them - able to navigate through even the most intense emotional storms with a sense of calm and purpose.

This clarity also enables you to let go of emotions that no longer serve you. Perhaps you've been carrying resentment or fear long after it was useful. As the funnel of R.E.S.T. strips away the unnecessary layers, you can release these emotions, understanding that they have fulfilled their role and are no longer needed. What remains is emotional clarity - a profound sense of peace, knowing that you're no longer weighed down by emotional baggage that belongs to the past.

Deepening Your Understanding of Trauma

The journey through the R.E.S.T. Pathway is more than a method of healing; it's a transformative experience that reshapes how you understand trauma and its role in your life. Trauma distorts everything: your perception of the world, your self-image, and your sense of what's possible. It's like looking at your reflection in a shattered mirror - each fragment shows a version of yourself that feels damaged, incomplete, or broken beyond repair. Trauma whispers to you that the worst moment of your life is the one that defines you. But through the R.E.S.T. model, you learn that trauma is not the end of your story - it's merely a chapter in the larger narrative of your life.

Initially, trauma feels overwhelming. It infiltrates every corner of your identity, leaving little room for anything else. You may find yourself replaying the painful memories, trapped in a cycle where it seems like the trauma is the only thing that matters. But as you move through the R.E.S.T. Pathway, you start to peel back the layers of unprocessed emotion, distorted beliefs, and outdated narratives that have kept you anchored in the past. Each phase of the funnel - Release, Examine Through Time, Select What Matters, and Transform Meaning - helps you shed the emotional baggage that weighs you down, revealing a deeper, more nuanced understanding of your trauma.

As you navigate these phases, you come to realize that trauma isn't just one thing. It isn't a monolithic force that consumes every part of who you are. Instead, trauma contains layers - some filled with pain and loss, yes, but others filled with growth, resilience, and even wisdom. This shift in perspective doesn't happen overnight. It unfolds gradually as you work through the funnel, gaining clarity and distilling your trauma down to its essential lessons.

You begin to see that, while trauma has undeniably shaped parts of your life, it does not define you. You are not solely the pain you've experienced; you are the strength you've built in its wake, the compassion you've learned to show yourself, and the wisdom you've gained through struggle. Trauma becomes a chapter in the book of your life, but it is not the book itself.

This process of discovery is not only liberating - it's deeply empowering. You start to reclaim the parts of yourself that trauma tried to take away. You realize that while trauma has left its mark, it has also revealed an unexpected depth within you: a capacity to heal, to grow, and to move beyond your circumstances. You become more than just a survivor; you become someone who has harnessed the transformative power of adversity.

Letting Go of Distorted Beliefs

At the heart of trauma lie distorted beliefs - those insidious thoughts that take root in the aftermath of pain. These beliefs often feel like truths because they emerge from your raw, emotional response to the trauma. Thoughts like, "I'm not worthy of love," "The world is unsafe," or "I'll never be whole again" become deeply ingrained because they seem to explain why the trauma happened. But these beliefs are more like survival mechanisms than actual reflections of reality. They are created to protect you, to make sense of a world that no longer feels stable or predictable.

As you move through the R.E.S.T. Pathway, particularly in the phase of Select What Matters, you begin to challenge these beliefs. Select What Matters asks you to step back and examine each belief with fresh eyes: "Does this belief truly serve me? Is it helping me move forward, or is it keeping me stuck in a narrative of fear and limitation?" This phase cuts through the emotional noise, helping you discern what is essential from what is simply a remnant of your trauma.

These beliefs often feel like immovable parts of your identity, but as you continue to work through the funnel, you start to realize that they don't belong to you anymore. They are relics of a time when you needed them to survive, but they no longer align with the person you're becoming. Letting go of these distorted beliefs is not easy. It's a process that takes time and patience, like slowly decluttering an attic filled with old, outdated relics. But as you clear away the emotional clutter, you make room for new, more empowering narratives.

The act of letting go is not about erasing your past or denying your pain. It's about releasing the limitations that keep you small and fearful. When you finally release these beliefs, you're not left with emptiness - you're left with clarity. You begin to see yourself not as broken or damaged, but as someone who has grown through adversity. The core truths that remain after this process reflect your resilience, your strength, and your capacity to heal. These truths become the foundation upon which you can rebuild your life - stronger, more aligned with who you truly are, and free from the distorted beliefs that once held you captive.

Gaining Emotional Clarity

The R.E.S.T. Pathway is not only about healing - it's about gaining emotional clarity. Trauma has a way of clouding your inner world, making it hard to distinguish between what is real and what is a product of fear, pain, or past experiences. When you are in the thick of trauma, everything feels overwhelming, and it's difficult to know where to focus your attention. The more you engage with the funnel, however, the clearer things become.

As you continue the practice of Release, Time-Based Reframing, Select What Matters, and Transform Meaning, the emotional noise begins to quiet. You start to understand the difference between your immediate, reactive emotions and the deeper, lasting truths that guide your healing. The fog of unresolved feelings and misplaced guilt begins to lift, and you can see which emotions deserve your attention and which are merely echoes of the past.

This clarity doesn't come from avoidance. It comes from actively facing your emotions, processing them, and then letting them go when they no longer serve you. The daily practice of releasing emotional reactivity creates space for peace to enter your life. You no longer feel overwhelmed by the intensity of your emotions because you've learned how to prioritize what matters and let go of what doesn't.

In this emotional clarity, you find a new sense of peace. You've created space for yourself to breathe, to reflect, and to move forward without being weighed down by the burdens of the past. You are no longer held captive by every passing emotion. Instead, you are grounded, centered, and able to approach each new day with a sense of purpose and balance.

Reclaiming Your Power

One of the most transformative aspects of the R.E.S.T. Pathway is that it enables you to reclaim your power. Trauma often makes you feel powerless, as though your life is no longer in your control. It can feel like the trauma has stolen your sense of agency, leaving you a passive observer in your own life. But as you work through the funnel, you start to see that you have more power than you ever realized. You have the power to choose how you respond to your trauma, to decide which beliefs you hold onto, and to determine what role your trauma will play in your life moving forward.

This realization is a turning point. It shifts the narrative from one of victimhood to one of resilience. You are no longer defined by what happened to you - you are defined by how you rise from it. This doesn't mean that the pain disappears or that the trauma is somehow justified. It means that you are reclaiming the parts of yourself that trauma tried to take away. You are rewriting the story, not as someone who was broken by trauma, but as someone who grew through it.

Moving Forward with Purpose

The R.E.S.T. Pathway is not just about healing from the past; it's about moving forward with purpose. As you shed the layers of emotional weight, distorted beliefs, and outdated narratives, you are left with a clearer sense of who you are and where you want to go. You begin to see that your trauma, while painful, has given you something valuable. It has deepened your empathy, sharpened your insight, and expanded your capacity for growth.

This newfound purpose is not about denying the pain or pretending that everything is fine. It's about integrating the trauma into the larger story of your life in a way that empowers you. It's about taking the lessons you've learned, the strength you've gained, and the clarity you've achieved and using them to move forward with intention and purpose.

In the end, the R.E.S.T. Pathway is a process of transformation. It helps you strip away what no longer serves you, refine your understanding of your trauma, and discover the core truths that will guide you into the next chapter of your life. It's not just about surviving your trauma - it's about transcending it, about becoming someone who is defined not by pain, but by resilience, wisdom, and an unshakeable sense of self. Through this journey, you reclaim your life, stronger and more aligned with your true self than ever before.

Discovering the Core Lessons of Trauma

As you continue to funnel down your daily experiences, emotional reactions, and distorted thoughts, what's left at the bottom are the core lessons your trauma has offered you. These are the truths you carry with you into the next phase of your life. For many survivors, these lessons revolve around themes like resilience, compassion, self-worth, and the fragility of life.

What's important to remember is that these core lessons aren't static - they evolve as you continue to apply the R.E.S.T. model in your daily life. As you grow, heal, and face new challenges, the funnel continues to refine your understanding, helping you access even deeper layers of meaning and insight. The lessons that trauma teaches you are not merely scars - they are guideposts that lead you toward a richer, more meaningful life.

Carrying Core Truths into the Future

The ultimate goal of the R.E.S.T. model is to leave you with a clear, distilled understanding of the lessons trauma has taught you - lessons that you can carry with you into every new chapter of your life. These core truths act as anchors - guiding you through future challenges, reminding you of your strength, and providing a sense of purpose and direction.

Rather than being defined by your trauma, you are defined by the wisdom it has given you. The core lessons you carry forward are not a reminder of pain, but of growth. They serve as a testament to your resilience, your ability to heal, and your capacity to create meaning from even the most difficult experiences. Through the R.E.S.T. process, you continually refine and deepen these core truths, allowing them to guide you through life with clarity, strength, and peace.

Long-Term Resilience: Living the R.E.S.T. Method

Resilience in trauma recovery is not about never feeling pain again or eliminating all signs of suffering. It's about the ability to adapt, reflect, and grow. It's about facing new challenges with a clearer, stronger sense of self and purpose. The R.E.S.T. model equips you with tools that can be applied not only to your past trauma but to any future difficulties you may encounter. By continuing to use the principles of Release, Integrate, Select What Matters, and Transform Meaning, you'll find yourself grounded, aware of your priorities, and able to derive meaning from every experience.

Your trauma is a part of you, but it does not define you. Through the R.E.S.T. model, you learn to transcend it - not by erasing it, but by changing how it lives within you. By incorporating the R.E.S.T. model into your daily life, you transform healing into a lifelong practice, a continual unfolding of resilience, growth, and deeper understanding.

The End of the Funnel, the Beginning of Renewal

Transform Meaning is the point where the R.E.S.T. model becomes truly transformative. It's the bottom of the funnel, where all the emotional clutter, distorted beliefs, and unnecessary burdens have been stripped away. What remains is you - your core, your purpose, and your meaning in life. Trauma may have shaped parts of your journey, but it no longer controls your narrative. Through the R.E.S.T. model, you learn to integrate your trauma into a larger story - a story of strength, resilience, and growth.

Living with Transform Meaning is about continually renewing yourself. It's about facing life's challenges with a clear mind, an open heart, and a strong spirit. Long-term resilience isn't a distant goal; it's something you practice every day, refining your core and using every experience as an opportunity for growth. Through the R.E.S.T. Pathway, you come to realize that you are not your trauma. You are your growth.

R.E.S.T. Practice

Applying The R.E.S.T. Method in Practice

This chapter shows how the full pathway works as a continuing practice rather than a single insight.

Release: What needs to settle before you analyze this?

____

____

____

____

Examine Through Time: How might this feel or look different with time, distance, and support?

____

____

____

____

Select What Matters: What truly deserves your energy here?

____

____

____

____

Transform Meaning: What meaning can be built without minimizing what happened?

____

____

____

____

Reflection Prompts

- How do the four steps work together for one current challenge?

____

____

- Where do I usually skip the Release step?

____

____

- What would a full R.E.S.T. response look like this week?

____

____

Gentle Reminder

Do not force insight before your body has enough safety to hold it. Regulation comes before interpretation. You can return to any exercise slowly, briefly, and with support.

Daily Micro-Practice

The R.E.S.T. Method in Practice

Use this page as a brief daily practice. The point is repetition, not perfection. One honest sentence is enough.

Today I noticed:

____

____

____

____

The trauma-shaped story that appeared was:

____

____

____

____

The R.E.S.T. response I want to practice is:

____

____

____

____

One gentle action I can take next is:

____

____

____

____

Chapter 9

R.E.S.T. Daily: Making Healing a Way of Life

Embedding Healing into Everyday Life

Healing from trauma is not a linear process or a singular event, but rather an ongoing journey that evolves over time. Trauma leaves deep imprints, and while the pain may lessen, the scars are permanent reminders. But within these scars, there is also strength. Every day offers an opportunity to continue healing, to foster resilience, and to turn those reminders of pain into symbols of growth. This is where the R.E.S.T. model truly comes into play - not just as a framework for addressing trauma, but as a guide for living a life rooted in healing and empowerment.

In this chapter, we focus on how to integrate the principles of R.E.S.T. - Release, Examine Through Time, Select What Matters, and Transform Meaning - into your daily routine. It's about taking what you've learned and making it part of your everyday life, so that healing becomes not just something you work on in moments of crisis, but a continual practice of self-care, growth, and transformation.

Healing as a Lifelong Journey

When we think about healing from trauma, it's tempting to imagine a definitive end point - a day when the pain, fear, and memories simply fade away. But in reality, trauma recovery is not about reaching a destination where everything is "fixed." Trauma changes you, and while the intensity of its impact may diminish over time, its effects can last a lifetime.

But this doesn't mean you are forever bound by the weight of your trauma. Instead, healing is about learning how to carry that weight differently, to bear it with strength and grace. The R.E.S.T. model teaches that healing is a dynamic, evolving process. It doesn't end with the resolution of symptoms, but continues as you navigate life, encountering new challenges, joys, and setbacks.

Each day presents an opportunity to practice healing. The principles of R.E.S.T. offer a roadmap for this daily work - allowing you to integrate recovery into the fabric of your life, so that your trauma no longer defines or controls you. The more you engage with R.E.S.T. as a way of living, the more you cultivate a deep sense of empowerment and agency. You are no longer a passive survivor of your experiences, but an active creator of your healing journey.

Living with R.E.S.T. daily means approaching every moment, every interaction, with an awareness that you have the tools to heal, grow, and thrive. It means knowing that while trauma may be part of your story, it no longer dictates the course of your life.

Sustaining R.E.S.T. Practices in Daily Life

Mindfulness as a Daily Ritual

At the core of the R.E.S.T. model is mindfulness - the practice of being fully present in the here and now, without judgment. Mindfulness is not just about meditation; it's a state of being that you can cultivate in every moment of your day. Trauma often pulls you out of the present, anchoring you in the pain of the past or the fear of the future. Mindfulness, on the other hand, grounds you in the present, reminding you that this moment is the only one you truly have control over.

Start small. Incorporate mindfulness into the mundane, everyday moments of your life. When you wake up in the morning, before your feet hit the floor, take a few moments to breathe deeply. Feel the air enter your lungs, and slowly exhale, releasing any tension. This simple act of conscious breathing sets the tone for your day, signaling to your body and mind that you are present, centered, and ready to move forward.

As you go through your morning routine, engage your senses fully. Notice the warmth of the shower, the smell of your coffee, the way the sunlight filters through the windows. These seemingly small moments, when approached with mindfulness, become opportunities to ground yourself and reconnect with your body.

Mindfulness also allows you to approach difficult emotions with greater clarity. When anxiety, fear, or anger arises, instead of pushing these feelings away or becoming overwhelmed by them, you can acknowledge them without judgment. By simply noticing the sensation in your body - tightness in your chest, quickened breath - you create space between yourself and the emotion. This space allows you to respond to the emotion in a healthier, more balanced way, rather than reacting impulsively.

The more you practice mindfulness, the more it becomes second nature, allowing you to carry a sense of peace and groundedness throughout your day, even in moments of stress or challenge. Over time, mindfulness transforms from a practice into a way of life, one that nurtures healing and emotional resilience.

Cognitive Reframing: A Daily Mindset Shift

Cognitive reframing is one of the most transformative tools available in the R.E.S.T. model. Trauma has a way of leaving behind deeply entrenched negative beliefs, beliefs that act like shadows, dimming the light on your ability to heal and thrive. These distorted thought patterns can dominate your internal dialogue, shaping the way you see yourself, your relationships, and the world around you. They are not merely passing thoughts, but automatic reactions born from the pain and fear of your trauma. "I'm not safe," or "I'll never be happy again," are common refrains for trauma survivors - statements that may seem true in the aftermath of overwhelming experiences, but that also deeply limit your capacity to heal.

What makes these thoughts so powerful is that they often feel irrefutable. Trauma has a way of distorting your perception, convincing you that the world is inherently dangerous, or that happiness and fulfillment are out of reach. These thought patterns, while understandable, serve to keep you trapped in cycles of pain, fear, and self-doubt. They reinforce the narrative that your trauma defines you, shaping not just your view of the past but also your expectations for the future. Cognitive reframing is about confronting these narratives head-on, questioning their validity, and actively reshaping them into healthier, more empowering stories.

But cognitive reframing isn't about sugar-coating your reality or pretending that everything is fine. It's not about ignoring the pain, trauma, or fear. Instead, it is about recognizing that, while trauma has been part of your journey, it doesn't get to control how you move forward. It's about reclaiming your power by changing how you relate to the trauma in the present and how you allow it to influence your future.

The Power of Awareness

The first step in cognitive reframing is becoming aware of your automatic thoughts. Often, these thoughts are so ingrained in your psyche that you may not even realize when they take over. Cognitive reframing starts with recognizing the moments when negative, distorted thoughts arise. This could happen in response to a trigger, a challenge, or even just a small setback in your day. It's about noticing the story your mind is telling you - whether it's about your ability to handle stress, your sense of worth, or your outlook on the future - and pausing long enough to question it.

For example, you might find yourself thinking, "I'll never be good enough," after a difficult conversation or "I'm always going to feel this pain," after a particularly hard day. These thoughts often appear automatically, surfacing from the deep well of your trauma. But here's the thing: Just because a thought arises doesn't mean it's true. Trauma has distorted your view, and cognitive reframing offers you the opportunity to rewrite the narrative.

The Power of Questioning: Is This Thought True?

The most powerful question in cognitive reframing is also the simplest: Is this thought true? This question acts as a mental flashlight, shining light on the dark corners of your thinking, illuminating where fear, pain, and trauma have skewed your perception. When you ask yourself if a thought is true, you are engaging your rational mind, pulling yourself out of the automatic emotional response and into a more objective space where you can evaluate the thought more clearly.

Let's say you find yourself thinking, "I'll never be happy again." This thought is born from the pain of your trauma, the sense that the joy you once had has been lost forever. But when you ask yourself, "Is this thought true?" you begin to realize that the future is not set in stone. Yes, happiness may feel out of reach in this moment, but that doesn't mean it's gone forever. The trauma has led you to believe this thought is an undeniable fact, but in reality, it's a perception shaped by pain.

Once you begin questioning your thoughts, you create space to introduce a more balanced perspective. For example, you might remind yourself, "I've felt joy before, and while it feels distant now, I know it's possible to feel it again in the future." This shift doesn't erase the pain of your trauma, but it does begin to weaken the hold that distorted thinking has on your mind.

Rewriting the Narrative: A New Inner Dialogue

Cognitive reframing is not just about questioning negative thoughts - it's about actively rewriting them. Trauma often traps you in a mental loop where fear, anger, and self-doubt dominate your internal dialogue. Cognitive reframing allows you to break that cycle by replacing disempowering thoughts with narratives that reflect resilience, strength, and self-compassion.

The process of rewriting the narrative requires patience and persistence. Every day, you are presented with opportunities to shift your mindset. The next time you find yourself spiraling into negative thinking - whether it's about your ability to handle stress, your relationships, or your worthiness - pause. Challenge the thought. Ask yourself if it's based in truth or if it's a reaction born from fear. Then, actively work to replace that thought with one that is more balanced and empowering.

For instance, if you catch yourself thinking, "I'm not capable of handling this," try reframing it to, "This is difficult, but I've faced challenges before and have found ways to overcome them." Or if you think, "I'm not worthy of love," remind yourself, "I am worthy of love and support, even when I feel vulnerable."

These reframed thoughts may feel foreign at first, but with practice, they become more familiar. Cognitive reframing is not about quick fixes or simple affirmations. It's about doing the hard work of confronting the narratives that have been shaped by trauma and rewriting them in a way that empowers you. The more you engage in this process, the more you'll notice a shift in your mindset, where resilience and self-compassion replace fear and self-doubt.

The Daily Practice of Reframing

Cognitive reframing is a practice, and like any practice, it requires consistency. Each day presents countless opportunities to engage in reframing, and the more you do it, the easier it becomes. Start with small, manageable steps. The next time you notice a negative thought surfacing, pause, take a deep breath, and ask yourself, "Is this thought true?" Then, choose to reframe it.

Over time, you'll notice that reframing becomes more automatic. You'll begin to catch negative thoughts as they arise, and instead of being swept up in them, you'll have the tools to challenge and reshape them. This process doesn't happen overnight, but with practice, it becomes part of your daily life.

Think of cognitive reframing as mental training. Just as you would strengthen a muscle through regular exercise, you strengthen your ability to challenge and reshape your thoughts through consistent practice. Each time you successfully reframe a thought, you're reinforcing new, healthier neural pathways in your brain, helping to weaken the old patterns of thinking that have kept you stuck.

Breaking Free from the Mental Traps of Trauma

Over time, cognitive reframing helps you break free from the mental traps that trauma creates. Those distorted beliefs - "I'm not safe," "I'll never be happy again," "I'm not worthy" - lose their power over you. They may still arise from time to time, but they no longer define your reality.

Instead, you begin to approach life's challenges with greater confidence and clarity. You understand that while trauma has shaped you, it does not have to control you. You have the power to change how you relate to your thoughts, your emotions, and your experiences.

Cognitive reframing shifts your inner dialogue from one of defeat to one of empowerment. It reminds you that while you cannot control everything that happens to you, you can control how you respond. And in that response, you find your strength, your resilience, and your capacity to heal.

Cognitive Reframing and the R.E.S.T. Method

Within the R.E.S.T. model, cognitive reframing is woven into every phase of healing. In the Release phase, reframing helps you let go of the emotional weight of trauma by challenging the beliefs that keep you stuck. In Time-Based Reframing, it helps you reimagine your relationship with time, understanding that while the trauma was part of your past, it doesn't define your future. In Select What Matters, it helps you focus on what truly matters, filtering out the noise of negative thinking that distracts from your healing. And in Transform Meaning, reframing allows you to find purpose in your pain, to rewrite your story in a way that honors both your struggles and your strength.

The power of cognitive reframing lies in its simplicity and its depth. It's a tool that can be used in every moment of your day, whether you're dealing with a difficult conversation, a moment of self-doubt, or a trigger that reminds you of your trauma. Each time you engage in cognitive reframing, you are reclaiming a piece of your power, rewriting a piece of your story, and moving one step closer to the healing and empowerment that R.E.S.T. offers.

Building Emotional Resilience: The Heart of R.E.S.T.

Resilience isn't a fixed trait you're born with; it's a quality you cultivate and strengthen, day by day, through the choices you make and the actions you take. It's not about never experiencing pain or difficulty - it's about how you rise each time you fall. Within the R.E.S.T. framework, building emotional resilience is a core component of healing. Every time you engage with the practices of R.E.S.T. - whether it's grounding yourself in the present moment, reframing a negative thought, or practicing mindfulness - you are strengthening your emotional resilience, layer by layer.

Emotional resilience is the ability to withstand adversity and bounce back from hardship, but it's more than just survival. It's about facing life's challenges with grace, compassion, and the knowledge that you have the inner resources to handle whatever comes your way. It's about trusting yourself to navigate pain and uncertainty while maintaining hope and strength. As you build this resilience, the power trauma once held over you begins to diminish. You stop viewing setbacks as insurmountable defeats and start seeing them as opportunities for growth, as moments to test and reaffirm your inner strength.

But building resilience is a practice, not a destination. The more you work on it, the stronger it becomes. Emotional resilience is not the absence of struggle; it's learning to navigate pain without being defined by it. And this is where the R.E.S.T. model excels - it teaches you that healing is not about avoiding pain, but about learning to move through it with wisdom, patience, and the understanding that every challenge is an opportunity to deepen your strength.

The Role of Self-Compassion in Resilience

An often overlooked but vital element of resilience is self-compassion. Trauma has a way of amplifying the inner critic, that voice inside your head telling you that you should be "healed by now" or that you're "not doing enough." It's the voice that questions your progress, criticizes your setbacks, and makes you feel as though you are failing at recovery. But here's the truth: healing is not a race, and setbacks are not failures - they are part of the journey.

Self-compassion is the antidote to this inner critic. It allows you to meet yourself where you are, with kindness and patience, rather than judgment. By practicing self-compassion, you create space for healing, even on the hardest days. You give yourself permission to struggle, to feel the weight of your pain, and to grow at your own pace. Resilience isn't about being perfect; it's about allowing yourself to be human. It's about recognizing that healing is messy and non-linear, but that doesn't mean you aren't making progress.

Each time you practice self-compassion, you are reinforcing the belief that you are worthy of care, that your struggles are valid, and that healing takes time. You allow yourself the grace to stumble and get back up again, knowing that resilience isn't about never falling - it's about how you rise after each fall.

Healing Through Human Connection

Trauma can fracture your sense of connection - not only with others but with yourself. It often isolates you, making you feel as though no one could possibly understand your pain. This disconnection breeds a sense of loneliness that can be deeply damaging to your healing process. You may find yourself withdrawing from relationships, either because you fear being hurt again or because you believe that your pain is too much for others to bear. But healing does not - and cannot - happen in isolation. Human connection is one of the most powerful forces for recovery.

The R.E.S.T. model emphasizes the importance of rebuilding trust and connection, both with others and with yourself. Healing relationships doesn't mean rushing to open up to everyone around you. It begins with small, intentional steps - allowing yourself to be vulnerable in safe, supportive spaces. These might be trusted friends, a therapist, or a support group, people who validate your experience and remind you that you are not alone in your pain.

Surrounding yourself with a network of individuals who uplift and encourage your healing is essential. These connections act as anchors, grounding you when the waves of trauma feel overwhelming. They remind you that your pain is shared and that others are walking similar paths to recovery. When you feel isolated, your support system becomes a lifeline, helping you remember that healing is not just possible but probable, especially within the context of community.

But just as important as rebuilding trust in others is rebuilding trust in yourself. Trauma can leave you feeling disconnected from your instincts, making you question your own emotions, decisions, and capabilities. By practicing mindfulness, grounding, and cognitive reframing, you slowly rebuild that trust. You learn to listen to your body's signals, to honor your needs, and to trust that you are capable of navigating life's challenges.

Rebuilding trust with yourself and others doesn't mean forcing yourself into vulnerability before you're ready. It's about knowing when to engage and when to protect your energy. It's about balancing your need for connection with your need for self-care, understanding that both are vital for long-term healing.

Creating a Future Beyond Trauma

The R.E.S.T. model teaches a powerful lesson: your trauma may have shaped you, but it doesn't have to dictate your future. Trauma often feels all-consuming, as if it has claimed not just your past but your present and future as well. But R.E.S.T. helps you break free from that narrative. Through each phase of the model, you're reminded that while trauma is part of your story, it doesn't define your entire life.

One of the most empowering aspects of R.E.S.T. is its focus on transformation - on moving beyond trauma and stepping into a future that you actively create. R.E.S.T. gives you the tools to shift your mindset from one of survival to one of thriving. It encourages you to set goals, both small and large, that align with the future you want to build.

Start by setting manageable, achievable goals that support your well-being. These don't have to be monumental tasks - commit to practicing mindfulness for ten minutes each morning, or to taking a walk outside each day. Each small step reinforces your ability to create positive change in your life. And with each success, no matter how small, you begin to build confidence in your ability to direct your future.

Over time, these small victories accumulate. As you accomplish your daily goals, you'll begin to set your sights higher. Maybe you'll rekindle an old passion, start a new project, or pursue a dream that trauma made you believe was out of reach. The point is that through the R.E.S.T. model, you are equipped not just to survive your trauma, but to thrive in a life filled with joy, purpose, and meaning. You are no longer defined by your past - you are empowered to create a future of your choosing.

Embracing R.E.S.T. as a Way of Life

The R.E.S.T. model is more than just a framework for trauma recovery; it's a philosophy for living. It offers a way of seeing and experiencing life that empowers you to face challenges with resilience, navigate uncertainty with grace, and embrace healing as an ongoing, dynamic process. It's a reminder that you are constantly evolving, rising higher with each experience, whether joyful or painful. As you integrate mindfulness, cognitive reframing, emotional resilience, and grounding techniques into your daily routine, these practices become second nature. They transcend their initial purpose as tools for coping with trauma, blossoming into habits that nurture your well-being, guide your growth, and support your ongoing journey of transformation.

Living with R.E.S.T. means recognizing that healing is not a linear path with a distinct endpoint. It's not about reaching a final destination where all wounds are neatly healed and tucked away. Healing is a continuous, lifelong process - one that grows with you as you evolve, one that deepens with every new experience. Each challenge you face becomes an opportunity to practice what you've learned through R.E.S.T., whether it's responding to stress with mindfulness, reframing a negative thought, or grounding yourself in the present moment. These are not one-off solutions; they are building blocks of a resilient, meaningful life.

The Evolution of Healing: From Survival to Growth

In the beginning, R.E.S.T. might have felt like a lifeline - a set of techniques to help you cope, survive, and manage the overwhelming emotions of trauma. But as you've practiced and integrated its principles, something powerful has shifted. These tools are no longer just mechanisms to help you survive; they are the keys to thriving. They have evolved from being a response to pain into a proactive way of living, helping you create a future built not on fear but on strength, resilience, and intention.

Mindfulness, for instance, once might have been a way to calm your racing thoughts or ground yourself during moments of anxiety. Now, it's more than just a tool - it's a way of seeing the world. It allows you to be present, fully engaged in each moment, no longer consumed by the shadows of the past or worries about the future. Cognitive reframing, which initially helped you challenge distorted beliefs shaped by trauma, now empowers you to approach every situation with an open mind and a balanced perspective. You've developed the ability to reframe not just your past, but your present and future, seeing each challenge as an opportunity for growth rather than as a threat.

Healing as a Continuous Journey

Living with R.E.S.T. means embracing healing as an ongoing, ever-evolving journey. There is no final chapter in the story of your healing, just as there is no single peak in the mountain range of life. Healing is not a box to be checked or a list of tasks to be completed before declaring yourself "healed." Rather, healing grows with you, adapting to new circumstances, deepening with each new layer of self-discovery, and unfolding over time as you continue to rise.

There will still be challenges - moments when old feelings resurface, when the weight of past wounds reappears in unexpected ways. But now, with R.E.S.T. as your foundation, these moments are no longer paralyzing. Instead, they are opportunities for deeper reflection and renewed growth. You are equipped to respond, not react. The mindfulness practices you've honed allow you to breathe through the tension, to ground yourself in the present, to remind yourself that you have risen before and can rise again. The cognitive reframing techniques you've learned empower you to reframe these moments, not as setbacks, but as steps along the winding road of healing.

With R.E.S.T., each experience becomes a chance to reaffirm your strength, to practice the skills that have brought you this far, and to continue evolving into the person you are becoming. The journey isn't about arriving at some perfect state of being; it's about recognizing that healing, growth, and resilience are part of the fabric of your life. You are always rising - higher, stronger, and more connected to yourself and others.

Reclaiming Power Through R.E.S.T.: You Are the Author of Your Story

At the core of R.E.S.T. is the radical idea that no matter what has happened to you, you are in control of how your story unfolds from here. Trauma may have once dictated your narrative, overshadowing your thoughts, your actions, and your sense of self. But through R.E.S.T., you've reclaimed the pen. You've learned that while you couldn't control what happened to you, you can absolutely control how you respond, how you grow, and how you move forward.

Every mindful breath you take, every reframed thought you practice, every act of resilience is a step toward reclaiming your power. With R.E.S.T., you're no longer living in reaction to the trauma - you're living in creation of your future. You are actively writing new chapters in your life, ones that reflect the courage, hope, and strength you've cultivated. Trauma no longer holds the pen in your life's story. You do.

This reclamation of power is not about erasing the past. It's about owning your narrative. It's about seeing yourself not as a victim of circumstance, but as a resilient, empowered individual who has the capacity to move beyond even the darkest moments. With R.E.S.T., you have not only survived your trauma - you've transcended it. You've turned your wounds into wisdom, your pain into power, and your struggles into sources of growth.

Living with Intention: Setting the Course for Your Future

Embracing R.E.S.T. as a way of life means living with intention. It means consciously deciding how you want to show up in the world, how you want to engage with yourself and others, and how you want to navigate life's complexities. Living with intention is about making mindful choices that align with your values, your purpose, and your goals. It's about asking yourself: What kind of life do I want to create moving forward?

This question goes beyond the immediate process of trauma recovery. It's a question that guides your every decision, your every action. Do you want to cultivate deeper, more meaningful relationships? Do you want to prioritize self-care and inner peace? Do you want to find ways to contribute to the world that feel aligned with your values? These are the kinds of questions that living with intention requires you to consider.

Intentions aren't about perfection. They aren't rigid goals that you must achieve at all costs. Instead, they are the guiding principles that help you live in alignment with your true self. They offer a sense of direction, a path to follow as you navigate the ups and downs of life. With R.E.S.T., you've developed the skills to set these intentions and to follow through on them, even when challenges arise.

Resilience: A Practice, Not a Destination

Resilience is not something that you achieve and then move on from. It's a practice - a daily commitment to move beyond adversity, to adapt to change, and to grow through challenges. R.E.S.T. has given you the tools to build resilience, but living with resilience requires continuous practice. Each day presents new opportunities to reinforce the habits of resilience you've developed.

Living with R.E.S.T. means practicing resilience in small ways, every day. It means grounding yourself when stress arises, reframing negative thoughts when they surface, and returning to the present moment when your mind starts to wander into fear or worry. These daily practices are not about perfection - they are about persistence. They are about showing up for yourself, again and again, even when it's hard.

Through these practices, resilience becomes more than just a response to difficulty. It becomes a way of living that allows you to navigate life's complexities with grace. It enables you to face challenges not with dread or fear, but with a sense of empowerment, knowing that you have the strength and the tools to move beyond whatever comes your way.

The Ripple Effect: Healing Through Connection

Trauma often isolates us. It creates barriers between us and the people we care about, and sometimes even between us and ourselves. But as you've learned through R.E.S.T., healing doesn't happen in isolation. It happens through connection - connection to yourself, to others, and to the world around you.

Living with R.E.S.T. means embracing connection as a vital part of your ongoing healing journey. It means reconnecting with yourself - learning to trust your instincts, listen to your emotions, and honor your needs. It means fostering relationships that are supportive, nurturing, and aligned with your values. And it means engaging with the world in ways that feel meaningful and purposeful.

As you continue to live with R.E.S.T., you'll find that these connections deepen. The relationships you build will be more authentic, more fulfilling, and more rooted in mutual respect and understanding. You'll also find that your connection to yourself grows stronger, allowing you to trust your inner wisdom and make decisions that align with your true self.

The Future You're Creating: A Life of Purpose and Joy

The ultimate goal of R.E.S.T. is not just to help you recover from trauma but to guide you toward a life of purpose, joy, and fulfillment. Trauma may have been a part of your past, but it does not have to dictate your future. With R.E.S.T., you've learned to reclaim your power, reshape your narrative, and move beyond the challenges life has thrown your way.

As you move forward, remember that living with R.E.S.T. is about embracing the fullness of life. It's about experiencing both the joys and the challenges with a sense of resilience and purpose. It's about knowing that you have the strength to rise, no matter what comes your way. With the tools of R.E.S.T., you are not just surviving - you are thriving. You are creating a life that reflects the wholeness of who you are, a life that is filled with passion, creativity, love, and connection.

This is your new beginning. You are no longer defined by your trauma - you are defined by your ability to move beyond it. And as you continue to rise, you are creating a future filled with endless possibilities for growth, love, and joy.

Embrace this journey with open arms. You are ready to rest, rebuild, and move forward.

R.E.S.T. Practice

Applying R.E.S.T. Daily: Making Healing a Way of Life

This chapter turns the method into daily rhythms, reflection, awareness, and small acts of restoration.

Release: What needs to settle before you analyze this?

____

____

____

____

Examine Through Time: How might this feel or look different with time, distance, and support?

____

____

____

____

Select What Matters: What truly deserves your energy here?

____

____

____

____

Transform Meaning: What meaning can be built without minimizing what happened?

____

____

____

____

Reflection Prompts

- What daily rhythm could support my healing?

- What small practice can I repeat without overwhelming myself?

- How can I measure progress gently rather than perfectly?

Gentle Reminder

Do not force insight before your body has enough safety to hold it. Regulation comes before interpretation. You can return to any exercise slowly, briefly, and with support.

Daily Micro-Practice

R.E.S.T. Daily

Use this page as a brief daily practice. The point is repetition, not perfection. One honest sentence is enough.

Today I noticed:

____

____

____

____

The trauma-shaped story that appeared was:

____

____

____

____

The R.E.S.T. response I want to practice is:

____

____

____

____

One gentle action I can take next is:

____

____

____

____

Chapter 10

Transcending Trauma: The Life You Are Rebuilding

Thriving Beyond Trauma: Embracing a New Beginning

As you reach this final chapter, take a deep breath and reflect on how far you've come. The road to healing from trauma is one of the most difficult journeys a person can undertake. It requires an immense amount of strength, courage, and persistence. But as you stand at the edge of this new beginning, having walked the path of recovery with the R.E.S.T. model as your guide, you are not just surviving - you are thriving.

This moment marks a turning point. The trauma that once felt all-encompassing has loosened its grip. The emotional weight that once held you down no longer defines your every thought and feeling. Instead, you are stepping into a future where you are no longer tethered to the past, where your experiences have shaped you but no longer confine you. You are entering a phase of life that is yours to shape, filled with hope, resilience, and a newfound sense of purpose.

The R.E.S.T. model - Release, Examine Through Time, Select What Matters, and Transform Meaning - has provided you with the tools to heal, rebuild, and grow. It has taught you how to release the emotional grip of trauma, to reframe your thoughts, and to find a deeper sense of meaning. But more than that, R.E.S.T. has equipped you with a framework that extends far beyond trauma recovery itself. It's not just a set of steps to move beyond the past, but a way of living that enables you to continually rise - no matter what challenges life presents.

Standing at the Crossroads: A New Beginning Awaits

As you stand here today, you are at the crossroads between your past and your future. Trauma, at one point, might have felt like a defining chapter in your life. It shaped how you viewed yourself, how you interacted with others, and how you navigated the world around you. But now, after walking through the steps of R.E.S.T., you've learned that trauma doesn't get to write your final chapter. The future you are stepping into is not confined by the past - it is open, expansive, and full of possibility.

What lies ahead of you now is a journey of growth, a life where resilience is your foundation and joy is your destination. You've done the difficult work of confronting your trauma, processing your pain, and reframing the narratives that once held you captive. Now, it's time to thrive. To embrace a future that is no longer bound by the wounds of yesterday but enriched by the strength you've cultivated through healing.

Reflecting on Your Journey: The Strength of Survival

Before looking ahead, it's important to take a moment to reflect on the journey that has brought you here. Healing from trauma is not a linear process. It's a winding road filled with highs and lows, breakthroughs and setbacks, moments of clarity, and moments of doubt. And yet, you've made it through.

Think back to where you started - the confusion, the overwhelming emotions, and the unbearable weight of the past that once clouded every aspect of your life. At that time, it might have felt impossible to break free from the cycle of fear, anxiety, or grief that seemed to define you. Yet, step by step, with the help of the R.E.S.T. model, you began to release the weight of those feelings. You learned how to ground yourself in the present, to distance yourself from the emotional flashbacks, and to regain control over your mind and body.

R.E.S.T. taught you that healing is not about erasing the past, but about reshaping how it lives within you. Through the practice of cognitive reframing, you began to see the events of your past in a new light - not as defining scars but as experiences that have contributed to your growth. Each tool you've learned - whether it was grounding exercises, mindfulness, or reframing negative thoughts - became an integral part of your healing journey. They helped you regain control, not just temporarily, but for the long term.

As you reflect on this progress, give yourself credit. Too often, we focus on what's still left to do, overlooking how far we've already come. Your journey through R.E.S.T. has been one of growth, resilience, and transformation. You didn't just survive your trauma - you've transformed because of it. You are stronger, wiser, and more capable than you were before.

Empowerment Through R.E.S.T.: Owning Your Story

Empowerment isn't something that happens overnight, nor is it something that can be given to you by someone else. Empowerment is something you cultivate within yourself, and through R.E.S.T., you've done exactly that.

There was a time when trauma dictated your thoughts, emotions, and actions - when it felt as though you were a passive participant in your own life, constantly reacting to the world around you. The fear, anxiety, and sadness felt inescapable, and you may have wondered if you'd ever regain control. But with each step you've taken in your healing process, you've reclaimed that control. You've learned that while you couldn't control what happened to you, you can absolutely control how you respond to it.

Through R.E.S.T., you've taken ownership of your story. You've redefined the narrative from one of victimhood to one of strength and resilience. Each time you faced a trigger and grounded yourself in the present, each time you reframed a negative thought or practiced select what matters, you were reclaiming power over your mind and body. You've learned to trust yourself again, to make decisions based on the person you are today rather than the fear and pain of the past.

This empowerment is profound. It's the understanding that you are no longer living in reaction to the trauma - you are actively creating the life you want. Trauma no longer holds the pen in your life's story. You do. And with that power comes the freedom to define what comes next.

Setting Intentions for Your Future: Living with Purpose

As you look forward to this new phase of your life, it's important to set intentions for how you want to live moving forward. Healing from trauma isn't about returning to who you were before - it's about becoming someone stronger, more aware, and more aligned with your true self. Now, you have the opportunity to set intentions that reflect the person you've become and the future you wish to create.

Intentions are different from goals. They're not about achieving specific outcomes or ticking boxes off a checklist. Instead, intentions are about how you want to be in the world. They are rooted in values and purpose, guiding you toward a life that feels authentic and meaningful.

Start by asking yourself: What kind of life do I want to create moving forward? Perhaps you want to focus on cultivating deeper, more meaningful relationships, or maybe you want to prioritize self-care and personal growth. Maybe your intention is to embrace creativity, to pursue a long-held passion, or to find new ways to contribute to the world around you.

These intentions don't have to be grand or life-changing right away. They can be simple, daily actions that reflect your commitment to yourself. For example, you might set an intention to practice mindfulness every morning, to spend more time outdoors, or to reconnect with a hobby you once loved. Small, intentional actions can lead to profound changes over time, helping you align your life with your deepest values.

Transformation Through Resilience: The Power of Daily Practices

Resilience is not something that magically appears when life gets tough. It's something you build, piece by piece, through the choices you make every day. R.E.S.T. has given you the tools to build resilience, and now it's up to you to continue strengthening that foundation.

Every time you practice mindfulness, every time you ground yourself in the present, every time you reframe a negative thought, you are reinforcing your resilience. These daily practices are the threads that weave together a life of strength and stability. They help you stay centered when life throws challenges your way. They remind you that you are capable of navigating even the most difficult situations with grace.

But resilience isn't just about bouncing back from hardship. It's about growing through it. It's about understanding that pain is a part of life, but it doesn't have to define your life. It's about knowing that while you can't control everything that happens, you can control how you respond. Resilience is the ability to face life's inevitable struggles with the knowledge that you have the tools and inner resources to get through them.

Each day that you commit to these practices, you are building a life of resilience. You are creating a foundation that allows you to bend without breaking, to weather life's storms without being swept away. This is the power of R.E.S.T. - not just as a trauma recovery model, but as a way of living that supports you in every aspect of your life.

Healing Through Connection: Rebuilding Trust and Relationships

Trauma has a way of isolating us, severing our connections to others and, at times, to ourselves. It can make you feel like no one understands your pain or like the world is unsafe. But one of the most profound lessons of the R.E.S.T. model is that healing doesn't happen in isolation. Healing happens in connection - with others and with yourself.

Rebuilding trust is an essential part of thriving beyond trauma. This starts with reconnecting with yourself. Trauma can leave you feeling disconnected from your own instincts and emotions, making it difficult to trust your decisions or even your sense of reality. But through R.E.S.T., you've learned to rebuild that trust. Grounding techniques, mindfulness, and emotional regulation have taught you how to listen to your body's signals, how to honor your needs, and how to trust your inner wisdom.

As you continue to rebuild trust with yourself, you'll find that your relationships with others begin to heal as well. Trauma often creates barriers between you and the people you care about, leading to feelings of isolation or fear of vulnerability. But healing through connection means allowing yourself to be seen and supported in safe, nurturing relationships.

Surround yourself with people who support your healing journey - those who uplift and encourage you, who understand your need for boundaries and respect your emotional process. Whether it's a close friend, a family member, a therapist, or a support group, these relationships provide a sense of community that is vital to your ongoing recovery.

At the same time, it's important to recognize that rebuilding trust with others is a gradual process. It's not about rushing into relationships or forcing yourself to be vulnerable before you're ready. It's about learning when to open up and when to protect your energy, finding a balance between connection and self-care.

Embracing a Life of Purpose and Joy: Your New Beginning

The ultimate goal of R.E.S.T. is not just to help you recover from trauma but to guide you toward a life of purpose, joy, and meaning. Trauma may have been a defining part of your past, but it does not have to dictate your future. You have the power to create a life that reflects the fullness of who you are - one that is filled with passion, creativity, love, and connection.

As you move forward, remember that thriving beyond trauma is not about achieving a state of perfection or never experiencing pain again. It's about embracing the wholeness of life - its highs and lows, its beauty and its challenges - with the knowledge that you are resilient, capable, and strong. R.E.S.T. has given you the tools to navigate this journey, and now it's up to you to continue applying them in ways that feel authentic to you.

Each day is an opportunity to live with intention, to make choices that reflect your growth and your values. Whether it's pursuing a passion, building deeper connections, or simply finding moments of peace and joy, you have the ability to create a life that is meaningful and fulfilling.

This is your new beginning. It's a time to step into your power, to write the next chapter of your life with confidence and clarity. You are no longer defined by your trauma - you are defined by your ability to move beyond it. And in doing so, you are creating a future that is filled with endless possibilities for growth, love, and joy.

Embrace this new beginning with open arms. You are ready to move forward with steadiness, clarity, and meaning.

R.E.S.T. Practice

Applying Transcending Trauma: The Life You Are Rebuilding

This chapter brings the book toward integration: not forgetting what happened, but no longer letting it own the whole page.

Release: What needs to settle before you analyze this?

____

____

____

____

Examine Through Time: How might this feel or look different with time, distance, and support?

____

____

____

____

Select What Matters: What truly deserves your energy here?

____

____

____

____

Transform Meaning: What meaning can be built without minimizing what happened?

____

____

____

____

Reflection Prompts

- What part of my story is ready to be reclaimed?

____

____

- What future am I building beyond survival?

____

____

- What does transcending trauma mean in practical daily terms?

____

____

Gentle Reminder

Do not force insight before your body has enough safety to hold it. Regulation comes before interpretation. You can return to any exercise slowly, briefly, and with support.

Daily Micro-Practice

Transcending Trauma

Use this page as a brief daily practice. The point is repetition, not perfection. One honest sentence is enough.

Today I noticed:

____

____

____

____

The trauma-shaped story that appeared was:

____

____

____

____

The R.E.S.T. response I want to practice is:

____

____

____

____

One gentle action I can take next is:

____

____

____

____

Acknowledgments

First and foremost, I want to express my deepest gratitude to my incredible wife, Taylor Brown. Taylor, this book would not exist without your love, patience, and unwavering belief in me. Through the long nights, the moments of doubt, and the constant demands of this journey, you stood by me with unshakeable support. You've been my compass when I felt lost, my greatest advocate when I needed strength, and my steady foundation when the process seemed too heavy to carry alone. Your belief in this project, even when I questioned my own, has been the light that guided me through. I am endlessly grateful for you - for your love, your wisdom, and your encouragement. This book is as much yours as it is mine because, without you, none of this would have been possible.

To our two wonderful children, you are my greatest inspiration. Your laughter, curiosity, and boundless energy fill my life with purpose. Every day, you remind me of the importance of striving for a better, kinder, and more compassionate world. In many ways, this book is for you - born out of my desire to help build a world that is safer, more understanding, and more hopeful for your future. You've been my motivation to keep going, even on the hardest days, and I hope that the lessons and insights within these pages contribute, even in some small way, to a world where you can grow up feeling safe, loved, and full of possibility.

This book is dedicated to the three of you - Taylor, and our incredible children. You are the reason I push myself to be better every day, and the reason I want to contribute to something greater. This work is a reflection of that drive, and it is with all my love that I share it with the world.

Key Terms

R.E.S.T. Method: A four-part pathway for trauma recovery that helps readers Release emotional intensity, Examine pain through time, Select What Matters, and Transform Meaning.

Release: The practice of calming the emotional charge of trauma before trying to interpret, analyze, or reframe the experience.

Examine Through Time: A time-based reframing process that challenges the false permanence of pain by viewing present distress through past resilience, future possibility, and broader context.

Select What Matters: A values-based process of identifying what deserves emotional energy and releasing what trauma, guilt, shame, pressure, or fear taught the person to carry.

Transform Meaning: The process of building meaning after trauma without glorifying, excusing, or minimizing what happened.

False Permanence: The trauma-shaped belief that a current feeling, fear, or identity state will always remain as intense as it feels in the present moment.

Emotional Charge: The intensity of feeling that can make trauma-related thoughts feel urgent, absolute, or unquestionably true.

Meaning Without Minimizing: A healing stance that allows a person to create purpose and direction after pain without pretending the trauma was good, necessary, or deserved.

R.E.S.T. Worksheets

The Emotional Charge Check

What am I feeling right now?

____

____

____

____

Where do I feel it in my body?

____

____

____

____

How intense is it from 1 to 10?

____

____

____

____

What would help lower the intensity by one point?

____

____

____

____

The False Permanence Test

What pain or fear feels permanent today?

____

____

____

____

What evidence suggests this feeling may change over time?

____

____

____

____

What would my future self want me to remember?

____

____

____

____

What support would help me hold this more gently?

____

____

____

____

The Emotional Energy Audit

What am I carrying?

____

____

____

____

What truly belongs to me?

____

____

____

____

What was placed on me by trauma, fear, guilt, or pressure?

____

____

____

____

What deserves my energy now?

____

____

____

____

Meaning Without Minimizing

What happened that I refuse to excuse?

What did surviving this reveal about my strength or values?

What meaning can I build without calling the trauma good?

What future action reflects the person I am becoming?

References

Bremner, J. D. (2006). Traumatic stress: Effects on the brain. Dialogues in Clinical Neuroscience, 8(4), 445-461. This article examines how trauma affects brain structures such as the amygdala, hippocampus, and prefrontal cortex, providing neuroscientific backing for the long-term impacts of trauma on cognition and behavior.

Davis, D. M., & Hayes, J. A. (2011). What are the benefits of mindfulness? A practice review of psychotherapy-related research. Psychotherapy, 48(2), 198–208. This review highlights the effectiveness of mindfulness techniques in reducing anxiety, depression, and stress, emphasizing how integrating mindfulness into daily life can promote emotional regulation and resilience, as outlined in your R.E.S.T. model.

Foa, E. B., Keane, T. M., Friedman, M. J., & Cohen, J. A. (Eds.). (2009). Effective Treatments for PTSD: Practice Guidelines from the International Society for Traumatic Stress Studies (2nd ed.). Guilford Press. A comprehensive guide detailing evidence-based treatments for PTSD, including cognitive reframing and exposure therapy, validating the use of cognitive-based interventions to address the psychological impact of trauma.

Herman, J. L. (1997). Trauma and Recovery: The Aftermath of Violence - from Domestic Abuse to Political Terror. Basic Books. Judith Herman's seminal work on trauma and recovery delves into the stages of trauma healing and introduces methods that align with your R.E.S.T. model's framework, such as reclaiming power and purpose post-trauma.

Holzel, B. K., Lazar, S. W., Gard, T., Schuman-Olivier, Z., Vago, D. R., & Ott, U. (2011). How does mindfulness meditation work? Proposing mechanisms of action from a conceptual and neural perspective. Perspectives on Psychological Science, 6(6), 537–559. This article explores how mindfulness meditation affects brain function and structure, particularly in regions associated with self-regulation and emotional resilience, supporting the use of mindfulness in the healing process.

Kabat-Zinn, J. (2003). Mindfulness-based interventions in context: Past, present, and future. Clinical Psychology: Science and Practice, 10(2), 144-156. Jon Kabat-Zinn's work on mindfulness-based stress reduction (MBSR) demonstrates how mindfulness practices can alleviate suffering, reduce stress, and foster emotional healing in trauma survivors.

Levine, P. A. (2010). In an Unspoken Voice: How the Body Releases Trauma and Restores Goodness. North Atlantic Books. Peter Levine's exploration of somatic experiencing emphasizes how trauma is stored in the body and how practices like grounding (part of the R.E.S.T. model) can be effective in releasing trauma from the body's nervous system.

Neff, K. D. (2003). The development and validation of a scale to measure self-compassion. Self and Identity, 2(3), 223–250. This foundational study on self-compassion provides empirical support for the role of self-compassion in building resilience, reducing self-criticism, and promoting emotional healing - key components of trauma recovery.

Porges, S. W. (2011). The Polyvagal Theory: Neurophysiological Foundations of Emotions, Attachment, Communication, and Self-Regulation. W.W. Norton & Company. Stephen Porges' Polyvagal Theory provides insights into how trauma affects the autonomic nervous system and emphasizes the importance of self-regulation techniques, such as mindfulness and grounding, for trauma recovery.

Siegel, D. J. (2012). The Developing Mind: How Relationships and the Brain Interact to Shape Who We Are (2nd ed.). Guilford Press. Daniel Siegel's work integrates neuroscience, attachment theory, and mindfulness to explain how trauma affects brain development and interpersonal relationships, aligning with the themes of emotional resilience and healing through connection.

Van der Kolk, B. A. (2014). The Body Keeps the Score: Brain, Mind, and Body in the Healing of Trauma. Viking. Bessel van der Kolk's research on trauma's effects on the body and mind supports the use of mindfulness, cognitive reframing, and body-based therapies for effective trauma recovery, echoing principles within the R.E.S.T. model.